NITEHAWK
CINEMA
PRESENTS

NITEHAWK CINEMA PRESENTS

MOVIE-INSPIRED MENUS FROM BROOKLYN'S DINE-IN THEATER

The Countryman Press

An Imprint of W. W. Norton & Company
Independent Publishers Since 1923

Page 10: PictureLux / The Hollywood Archive / Alamy Stock Photo; 15: OFF WHITE PRODUCTIONS / Ronald Grant Archive / Alamy Stock Photo; 20: PictureLux / The Hollywood Archive / Alamy Stock Photo; 26: UNITED ARTISTS / AF archive / Alamy Stock Photo; 29: Ronald Grant Archive / Alamy Stock Photo; 32: COLUMBIA PICTURES / Ronald Grant Archive / Alamy Stock Photo; 35: PictureLux / The Hollywood Archive / Alamy Stock Photo; 38: RGR Collection / Alamy Stock Photo; 39: Sony Pictures / Entertainment Pictures / Alamy Stock Photo; 43: Elara Pictures / Moviestore Collection Ltd / Alamy Stock Photo; 46: Warner Brothers / Album / Alamy Stock Photo; 51: Pictorial Press Ltd / Alamy Stock Photo; 54: Warner Brothers / AF archive / Alamy Stock Photo; 7: ANNAPURNA PICTURES / Allstar Picture Library Ltd. / Alamy Stock Photo; 61: Warner Brothers / AA Film Archive / Alamy Stock Photo; 63: Photo 12 / Alamy Stock Photo; 68: PARAMOUNT PICTURES / Album / Alamy Stock Photo; 71: © Warner Brothers / Courtesy Everett Collection 72: Photo 12 / Alamy Stock Photo; 77: Warner Brothers / Pictorial Press Ltd / Alamy Stock Photo; 78: Pictorial Press Ltd / Alamy Stock Photo; 81: APL Archive / Alamy Stock Photo; 84: RGR Collection / Alamy Stock Photo; 88: Gallo Images / Foto24 / Denzil Maregele/Gallo/ Alamy Live New; 89: © Henry Chalafant '82 Skeme Tops Train; 94: Moviestore Collection Ltd / Alamy Stock Photo; 98: Moviestore Collection Ltd / Alamy Stock Photo; 101: Moviestore/Rex Features/Entertainment Pictures / Alamy Stock Photo; 102: United Archives GmbH / Alamy Stock Photo; 106: RGR Collection / Alamy Stock Photo; 110: JENS TRENKLER/dpa picture alliance/Alamy Live News/ Alamy Stock Photo; 113: Fine Line / Allstar Picture Library Ltd. / Alamy Stock Photo; 114: ScreenProd / Photononstop / Alamy Stock Photo; 117: Lifestyle pictures / Alamy Stock Photo; 118: AMERICAN INTERNATIONAL / Ronald Grant Archive / Alamy Stock Photo; 123: Photo 12 / Alamy Stock Photo; 126: MIRAMAX / Ronald Grant Archive / Alamy Stock Photo; 129: Photo 12 / Alamy Stock Photo; 132: Pictorial Press Ltd / Alamy Stock Photo; 135: THE FILM COMPANY / AF archive / Alamy Stock Photo; 141: LADD COMPANY/WARNER BROS / Album / Alamy Stock Photo; 153: MARKA / Alamy Stock Photo; 160: The Print Collector / Alamy Stock Photo; 168: Lifestyle pictures / Alamy Stock Photo; 171: Warner Brothers / Allstar Picture Library Ltd. / Alamy Stock Photo; 174: UIP / AA Film Archive / Alamy Stock Photo; 176: Photo 12 / Alamy Stock Photo; 183: Moviestore Collection Ltd / Alamy Stock Photo; 186: BFA / Toho Company / Alamy Stock Photo; 187: Photo 12 / Alamy Stock Photo; 190: Lifestyle pictures / Alamy Stock Photo; 193: Photo 12 / Alamy Stock Photo; 197: Photo 12 / Alamy Stock Photo; 200: Courtesy Everett Collection; 204: Historic Collection / Alamy Stock Photo; 207: COMPAGNIA CINEMATOGRAFICA CHAMPION / Cortesía Album / Album / Alamy Stock Photo; 211: UNIVERSAL PICTURES / Album / Alamy Stock Photo; 212: © Columbia Pictures / Courtesy Everett Collection; 212: Moviestore Collection Ltd / Alamy Stock Photo; 216: HKM FILMS / AF archive / Alamy Stock Photo ; 219: Pictorial Press Ltd / Alamy Stock Photo; 223: Moviestore Collection Ltd / Alamy Stock Photo; 226: IAC FILMS / Allstar Picture Library Ltd. / Alamy Stock Photo; 230: Pictorial Press Ltd / Alamy Stock Photo; 233: PictureLux / The Hollywood Archive / Alamy Stock Photo; 236: UNIVERSAL PICTURES /Allstar Picture Library Ltd. / Alamy Stock Photo; 239: UNIVERSAL / AA Film Archive / Alamy Stock Photo; 241: LUCASFILM / Allstar Picture Library Ltd. / Alamy Stock Photo; 242: WARNER BROS / Allstar Picture Library Ltd. / Alamy Stock Photo; 249: United Archives GmbH / Alamy Stock Photo; 252: © Judie Burstein/Globe Photos/ ZUMAPRESS.com / ZUMA Press, Inc. / Alamy Stock Photo; 255: Annapurna Pictures/Entertainment Pictures / Alamy Stock Photo; 263: BFA / CJ Entertainment / Alamy Stock Photo; 268: Magnolia Pictures / Alamy Stock Photo; 271: Entertainment Pictures / Alamy Stock Photo; 276: Photo 12 / Alamy Stock Photo; 279: WERNER HERZOG FILMPRODUKTION / Album / Alamy Stock Photo; 280: PARAMOUNT / Allstar Picture Library Ltd. / Alamy Stock Photo; 283: WARNER BROS / Allstar Picture Library Ltd. / Alamy Stock Photo; 287: MCA/UNIVERSAL /AA Film Archive / Alamy Stock Photo; 288: Masheter Movie Archive / Alamy Stock Photo; 292: Entertainment Pictures / Alamy Stock Photo; 295: Pictorial Press Ltd / Alamy Stock Photo; 299: Photo 12 / Alamy Stock Photo; 300: MARKA / Alamy Stock Photo; 303: SNAP/ Entertainment Pictures / Alamy Stock Photo; 304: Moviestore Collection Ltd / Alamy Stock Photo; 307: FOX SEARCHLIGHT / AA Film Archive / Alamy Stock Photo

For information about permission to reproduce selections from this book, write to Permissions, The Countryman Press, 500 Fifth Avenue, New York, NY 10110

For information about special discounts for bulk purchases, please contact W. W. Norton Special Sales at specialsales@wwnorton.com or 800-233-4830

Manufacturing by Versa Press
Book design by Allison Chi
Production manager: Devon Zahn

Library of Congress Cataloging-in-Publication Data

Names: Viragh, Matthew, author.
Title: Nitehawk Cinema presents Movie-inspired menus from Brooklyn's dine-in theater / Matthew Viragh.
Other titles: Movie-inspired menus from Brooklyn's dine-in theater
Description: New York : The Countryman Press, [2021] | Includes index.
Identifiers: LCCN 2021039198 | ISBN 9781682685945 | ISBN 9781682685952 (epub)
Subjects: LCSH: Cooking-New York (State)-New York. | Nitehawk Cinema (Dine-in theater) | LCGFT: Literary cookbooks.
Classification: LCC TX714 .V558 2021 | DDC 641.59747-dcundefined
LC record available at https://lccn.loc.gov/2021039198

The Countryman Press
www.countrymanpress.com

A division of W. W. Norton & Company, Inc.
500 Fifth Avenue, New York, NY 10110
www.wwnorton.com

10 9 8 7 6 5 4 3 2 1

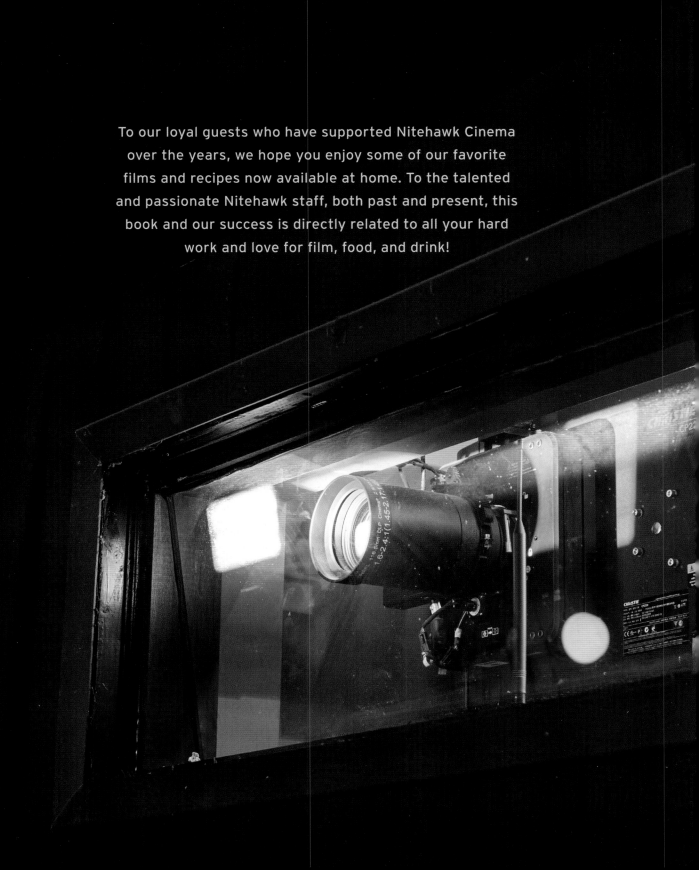

To our loyal guests who have supported Nitehawk Cinema over the years, we hope you enjoy some of our favorite films and recipes now available at home. To the talented and passionate Nitehawk staff, both past and present, this book and our success is directly related to all your hard work and love for film, food, and drink!

CONTENTS

INTRODUCTION

This book was designed to bring home our formula for combining food, film, and cocktails into a complete cinema experience, something we've been doing at our independent cinema in Williamsburg, Brooklyn, since 2011 and at our second location in Park Slope, Brooklyn, since 2018. We'll bring together our team's passion for proper cocktails, fine grub, and obsessive film programming in pursuit of a more modern film-going experience. And it's an experience that can happen at home too.

A quick background on our little cinema: We opened the summer of 2011, but before we could, there was only one thing standing in the way of our complete celluloid cuisine vision: an old New York State Prohibition law that banned the sale of alcohol in movie theaters. We thought our concept was DOA after initially learning about this law; however, we were not deterred and embarked on attempting to change the law. There were no guarantees, it was definitely a long shot, and we planned on opening whether the law changed or not. But the timing worked out perfectly: A month after our opening Nitehawk in June 2011, Governor Andrew Cuomo signed a bill allowing booze to be served with food in movie theaters throughout the state of New York. We were officially the first dine-in theater to open in the state.

Our talented team began creating one-of-a-kind movie events with food and drink concoctions that were completely unexpected in a movie theater. As our experience and reputation grew in Brooklyn, we decided it was time for expansion and we were lucky enough to secure a derelict, historic theater right along Prospect Park (the Central Park of Brooklyn). We spent two years lovingly restoring what was left of this 1928 beauty. Our second location opened in 2018 on a much grander scale, with seven screens versus our original three screens in Williamsburg, but with the same spirit, creativity, and intimate experience that we honed originally.

For most every first-run new-release film we feature at either location, and for select repertory events, our kitchen and bar teams create film-inspired specials to enhance the viewing experience. Over the years we've developed a hell of a repertoire, and some of our favorites are being made available to you at home in this book. We have you covered for a potluck movie-screening party or just a quiet night at home, so have a look and get inspired. And let's Nitehawk and chill.

NOTE ON EQUIPMENT

These tools of the trade will serve you well in any home and are the baseline equipment list! Anything outside the following tools will be called out at the top of each individual recipe.

BAR

16-ounce pint glass
blender
cocktail barspoon
dropper bottle
fine cone strainer
fruit peeler
Hawthorne strainer
jiggers: 1 ounce, 2 ounces
julep strainer
mixing tin
muddler
standard cocktail set

KITCHEN

circular cutters
digital thermometer that reads
  up to 400°F
Dutch oven or slow cooker
immersion blender
knife
measuring cups
measuring spoons
mixing bowls
sieve
spatula (preferably rubber)
stand mixer
stovetop pots and pans
whisk

NOTE ON ALLERGIES

Food recipes or food-containing drink recipes that may include any of the food allergens currently identified as being the most common food allergies in the United States—dairy, eggs, fish, gluten, peanuts, shellfish, soy, or tree nuts—are flagged as such. Whether or not you find them among the so-called "Big Eight Allergens," please avoid any ingredients to which you are allergic.

Please note that grain-based alcoholic beverages may contain trace amounts of gluten, depending on their grain base or the manufacturing process; wine may have been clarified with albumin (egg) or chitosan (shellfish). If these allergens are of concern, visit the distillery's website for more information.

NEW YORK:

WHERE IT ALL BEGAN

NYC's rich film history is as old as film itself. From *King Kong* to *West Side Story* to *Do the Right Thing* and beyond, these iconic films made in this iconic city highlighted the diverse eras and cultures of this living, breathing melting pot. NYC not only played a vital role as the backdrop to so many historic films but it is also a city with one-of-a-kind movie exhibition: from movie palaces of the past to current independent cinemas to rooftop screenings in Brooklyn, movies are part of the cultural fabric in NYC.

One of the more colorful eras in movie exhibition played out on the stretch of 42nd Street from Seventh to Eighth Avenue. On this famous block, there were once dozens of historic theaters and, in its heyday, in the 1950s and '60s, the block was ablaze with marquee lights. It's where everyone and anyone, scenesters and trendsetters, went for a flick. Eventually the block, a marquee alley of sorts, followed the downward trend of NYC in the 1970s and '80s, becoming known as "The Deuce" after the glitz faded and the pimps and porno films moved in.

MS. CHEESECAKE | *PARIS IS BURNING (1990)*

CHEESECAKE BALLS IN THREE CATEGORIES: PEANUT AND BANANA, TUXEDO, AND COOKIE CRUMB, WITH CHAMPAGNE CARAMEL

YIELD: 20 BALLS
ALLERGIES: DAIRY, GLUTEN, PEANUTS
TOOL: 1-OUNCE SCOOP

Named after one of the categories of the drag queen balls in the film, "Ms. Cheesecake" means that "you must not only have a body, but you must also be sexy." Each type of cheesecake ball is dressed up for another category.

FOR THE CHEESECAKE

1 pound cream cheese

¾ cup confectioners' sugar

1 teaspoon lemon zest

5 tablespoons graham cracker crumbs

1 teaspoon vanilla extract

FOR THE PEANUT AND BANANA TOPPING

¼ cup chopped peanuts

¼ cup chopped banana chips

FOR THE TUXEDO TOPPING

4 ounces milk chocolate chips

4 ounces white chocolate chips

FOR THE COOKIE CRUMB TOPPING

¼ cup graham cracker crumbs

¼ cup chocolate sandwich cookie crumbs, such as Oreo

FOR THE CHAMPAGNE CARAMEL

½ cup Champagne

1 cup granulated sugar

¼ teaspoon salt

½ cup heavy cream

4 tablespoons (½ stick) unsalted butter

FOR GARNISH

Pop Rocks

TO MAKE THE CHEESECAKE

1. Place all the cheesecake ingredients in the bowl of a stand mixer fitted with the paddle attachment and mix until blended.

2. Allow to cool and firm in the refrigerator for at least 30 minutes, but more if possible.

3. Line a baking sheet with parchment paper and scoop 1-ounce balls of the chilled mixture onto the prepared pan.

4. Roll the balls with your hands to make them rounder.

5. Return the cheesecake balls to the refrigerator until ready to top.

TO MAKE THE PEANUT AND BANANA TOPPING

1. Stir together the peanuts and banana chips in a bowl.

2. Roll one-third of the balls in the mixture.

TO MAKE THE TUXEDO TOPPING

1. In a microwave-safe bowl, microwave the milk chocolate chips for 1 minute, stopping to stir every 15 seconds, until fully melted.

2. Dip one-third of the remaining balls halfway into the melted milk chocolate so that half of each ball is covered in chocolate.

3. Return the cheesecake balls to the refrigerator.

4. In a microwave-safe bowl, microwave the white chocolate chips for 1 minute, stopping to stir every 15 seconds, until fully melted.

5. Dip the other side of each ball in the melted white chocolate.

CONTINUED ▶

TO MAKE THE COOKIE CRUMB TOPPING

1. Stir the two kinds of cookie crumbs together in a bowl.
2. Roll the remaining cheesecake balls in the cookie crumb mixture.

TO MAKE THE CHAMPAGNE CARAMEL

1. Pour the Champagne into a heavy-bottomed saucepan, bring to a boil, and then lower the heat to a simmer.
2. Reduce by half.
3. In a separate saucepan, heat the heavy cream over low heat until warm.
4. Whisk the granulated sugar and salt into the reduced Champagne.
5. Cook the mixture until it reaches a light amber color, about 8 minutes.
6. Remove the Champagne sugar from the heat, and slowly and carefully pour in the cream, whisking constantly.
7. Whisk in the butter, $1\frac{1}{2}$ teaspoons at a time.
8. Allow to cool.

TO ASSEMBLE

1. Spoon the caramel onto a serving plate and spread with the back of a spoon across the plate.
2. Arrange the caramel with the cheesecake balls in your desired order.
3. Garnish with Pop Rocks.

The film documents the origins of "voguing," a dance style that became the subject of Madonna's 1990 worldwide hit music video, *Vogue*.

SUCK ON THIS! | *TAXI DRIVER* (1976)

WHISKEY, RYE TOAST, BLACKBERRY, ORANGE JUICE, LAPSANG SOUCHONG

YIELD: 1 SERVING
ALLERGIES: RYE, TREE NUTS (ALMOND)
GLASSWARE: COUPE GLASS

Driving a taxi cab all night, you never know what you're gonna get. So after you're done, you head to the diner, read the paper, grab a little buttered rye toast with jam, and head home. Sometimes you're accompanied by Jodie Foster—it's an unpredictable business; you never know!

1.5 ounces Two James Johnny Smoking Gun Whiskey

0.5 ounce fresh lemon juice

0.5 ounce Rye Toast Syrup (recipe follows)

0.25 ounce fresh orange juice

3 blackberries, muddled

0.25 ounce orgeat syrup (Small Hands Foods preferred)

Lapsang souchong tea for garnish

1. Combine all the ingredients, except the tea, in a mixing tin, add ice, and shake vigorously for 10 seconds, as if shaking a daiquiri.

2. Double strain into a chilled coupe glass.

3. Garnish with tea to form a small circle, à la every Scorsese character that gets a bullet through the cheek.

RYE TOAST SYRUP   YIELD: 15 TO 20 SERVINGS

1 cup organic rye berries

2 cups water

2 cups sugar

½ cup rye whiskey

1. Toast the rye berries in a medium saucepan over medium-high heat for 3 minutes, or until lightly toasted.

2. Add the water and boil for 20 minutes. Add the sugar.

3. Cook for an additional 10 minutes. Remove from the heat, add the rye whiskey, transfer to a blender, blend until smooth, then pass the mixture through a fine strainer.

If you can believe it, screenwriter Paul Schrader wrote the screenplay for *Taxi Driver* in just over one week. And author Fran Lebowitz, one of director Martin Scorsese's good friends in New York City, was probably the only female taxi driver in the 1970s, where she frequented the Belmore Cafeteria, the famed cabbie food stop featured in the film. In Scorsese's 2021 documentary, *Pretend It's a City*, Lebowitz said, "I remember *New York* magazine wrote an article like: Is this the best restaurant in New York because all these cab drivers eat here? And I remember thinking at the time, what would make you believe that the greatest judges of food would be cab drivers? When I was young, they used to say this is a great diner; the truck drivers eat here. Like these are the great connoisseurs of food. . . . They eat there because you can park, not a great recommendation for a restaurant necessarily." She recalled that her driver "colleagues" wouldn't acknowledge her existence during meals at the cafeteria.

ANYTIME, ANYWHERE | *TAXI DRIVER (1976)*

GYRO CHICKEN, AROMATIC RICE, HOT SAUCE, PITA

YIELD: 4 SERVINGS
ALLERGIES: DAIRY, GLUTEN
(IF SERVING WITH PITA)
TOOL: TONGS

Halal carts are ubiquitous around the city and are hubs for activity. Cabbies have their spots and take their breaks surrounding these carts. It can be a lonely existence, and the pit stops provide some opportunity to socialize.

FOR THE WHITE SAUCE

¾ cup mayonnaise

¾ cup plain Greek yogurt

1 teaspoon agave syrup

3 tablespoons apple
  cider vinegar

Zest and juice of 1 lemon

1 tablespoon minced fresh dill

2 teaspoons coarsely
  ground black pepper

1 tablespoon kosher salt

FOR THE RICE

2 tablespoons unsalted butter

¼ cup minced white onion

1 garlic clove, minced

1 tablespoon ground turmeric

1 teaspoon cumin seeds,
  toasted and ground

1 teaspoon coriander seeds,
  toasted and ground

1 cup uncooked basmati
  or jasmine rice

1⅔ cups chicken stock or water

Kosher salt and freshly
  ground black pepper

FOR THE CHICKEN

2 pounds boneless, skinless
  chicken thighs

Zest and juice of 4 lemons

3 tablespoons chopped
  fresh oregano

1 tablespoon coriander seeds,
  toasted and ground

1 tablespoon cumin seeds,
  toasted and ground

1 teaspoon ground sumac

Kosher salt and freshly
  ground black pepper

4 garlic cloves, crushed with
  the flat side of a chef knife

¼ cup olive oil

¼ cup canola or vegetable
  oil for cooking

FOR SERVING

Valentina hot sauce in
  a squeeze bottle

Tomato wedges

Shredded iceberg or
  romaine lettuce

Toasted pita bread

The modern NYC cabbie staple of the midshift lunch or dinner is the chicken over rice plate from their favorite halal cart.

TO MAKE THE WHITE SAUCE

1. Whisk all the white sauce ingredients together in a bowl until well combined.

2. Transfer to a squeeze bottle with a large tip.

3. Can be kept refrigerated for up to 4 days.

TO MAKE THE RICE

1. Melt the butter in a 2-quart saucepot over medium heat, add the minced onion and garlic, and sweat until translucent.

2. Once the onion and garlic are translucent, add the turmeric and the toasted and ground seeds. Let the spices warm through amid the onion mixture over medium heat.

3. Add the rice and toast along with the aromatics for 1 to 2 minutes.

CONTINUED ▷

4. Add the chicken stock or water, and season with salt and pepper. Cover the pot and bring to a boil.

5. Once the mixture comes to a boil, lower the heat to as low as possible. Cook for 15 minutes without stirring or removing the lid.

6. After 15 minutes, remove from the heat and let the rice rest for 1 to 2 minutes. Remove the lid and fluff the rice with a fork. Set the rice aside while you cook the chicken.

TO MAKE THE CHICKEN

1. Clean any excess fat or connective tissue from the chicken thighs.

2. Combine the lemon zest and juice, oregano, seeds, sumac, salt and pepper, garlic, and olive oil in a bowl and mix until smooth. Reserve half of the marinade in the refrigerator for later.

3. Place the remaining marinade in a large resealable plastic bag and add the chicken to marinate for a minimum of 1 hour but no more than 4 hours. Massage the chicken in the bag with the marinade every 30 to 45 minutes until ready to start cooking.

4. When ready to cook, heat a large cast-iron skillet over medium-high heat. Remove the chicken from the marinade (discard the used marinade) and pat dry with paper towels. Season with salt and pepper a second time.

5. When the skillet is hot, add the canola oil. Carefully place the chicken thighs in the oil-coated skillet and cook until browned on the first side. As the chicken is cooking on the first side, remove the reserved marinade from the refrigerator.

6. When the chicken is browned on the first side, flip with tongs, lower the heat to medium, and cook until the chicken reaches an internal temperature of 165°F.

7. When the chicken is cooked through, remove from the pan and let rest for 2 to 3 minutes. Roughly chop the chicken thighs into bite-size pieces. Return the chicken to the skillet with the remaining marinade and cook until the chicken is fully coated in the marinade.

TO SERVE

1. Place a scoop of the rice on a large dinner plate and top that with a quarter of the chicken pieces. In alternating lines, drizzle the top of the chicken with the white sauce and the Valentina hot sauce. Finish the plate with tomato wedges and shredded lettuce.

2. Serve the pita on the side.

GOOD BIRD | *BIRDMAN (2014)*

SPICY DILL CHICKEN WINGS, GARLICKY DILL YOGURT SAUCE, CARROT SLAW

YIELD: 6 TO 8 SERVINGS
TOOLS: BOX GRATER OR FOOD PROCESSOR

Celebrating the Bird persona, Riggan's artistic wings try to escape his career-defining comic book role and then ultimately allow his transformation into more. The yogurt and dill of his theatrical success become the perfect counter to the birdman-burn of jalapeño-spiced wings.

FOR THE CHICKEN WINGS

3 cups all-purpose flour
1 teaspoon garlic powder
1 teaspoon onion powder
2 teaspoons smoked paprika
½ teaspoon cayenne pepper
5 pounds chicken
 wings, patted dry
One 8-ounce bottle green
 Tabasco or other mild
 jalapeño hot sauce

Canola oil for frying
1 ounce fresh dill, minced

FOR THE YOGURT SAUCE

2 cups plain Greek yogurt
1 tablespoon minced fresh dill
2 tablespoons fresh lemon juice
1 tablespoon extra virgin olive oil
2 garlic cloves, minced
3 tablespoons water
1 tablespoon kosher salt

FOR THE CARROT SLAW

2 carrots, peeled
1 tablespoon Dijon mustard
2 tablespoons apple
 cider vinegar
¼ cup extra virgin olive oil
2 teaspoons kosher salt
½ teaspoon freshly
 ground black pepper
½ cup flat-leaf parsley, minced

TO MAKE THE WINGS

1. Combine the flour, garlic powder, onion powder, paprika, and cayenne in a bowl and set aside.

2. Toss the chicken wings in the green hot sauce in a separate bowl. Cover and let sit for at least 1 hour in the refrigerator.

3. Coat the wings with the seasoned flour.

4. Add the canola oil halfway up any tall-sided saucepot and heat to 350°F. Fry the wings in batches until they are golden brown and reach an internal temperature of 165°F.

5. As the wings are cooked through and come out of the oil, toss with the minced dill.

TO MAKE THE YOGURT SAUCE

While the wings are marinating, whisk together all the yogurt sauce ingredients in a bowl.

CONTINUED ▶

TO MAKE THE SLAW

1. Shred the carrots on the largest side of a box grater or in a food processor.
2. Whisk together the Dijon and vinegar in a small bowl. Slowly drizzle in the oil to emulsify into a vinaigrette. Season with the salt and pepper.
3. Toss the carrots with the vinaigrette, add the minced parsley, and season with salt and pepper.

TO SERVE

Serve the wings on top of the carrot slaw and garnish with the yogurt sauce to dip as needed.

Because the movie was carefully rehearsed, choreographed, and shot in sequence, editing was completed in two weeks. Only 16 cuts are visible in the film.

WE CAME WITH OUR HEARTS OPEN!

WEST SIDE STORY (1961)

GRANDMA SLICE–STYLE EMPANADILLAS

YIELD: 12 SERVINGS
ALLERGIES: EGG, GLUTEN
TOOL: ROLLING PIN

Drawing on New York City's rich tradition of immigrant foods combining and changing in unexpected and delicious ways, we've scooped up all the glory that is the grandma slice and put into one of Puerto Rico's most iconic street foods. *Mange* and *buen provecho!*

FOR THE DOUGH

3½ cups all-purpose flour, plus more for dusting
2 teaspoons baking powder
2 teaspoons salt
¼ cup vegetable shortening
1 large egg, beaten
¾ cup water

FOR THE FILLING

2 to 3 garlic cloves, minced
3 tablespoons olive oil
1 tablespoon chopped fresh parsley
Three 4-ounce balls fresh mozzarella
1 cup Sal's Famous Pizza Sauce, plus more for serving (page 27)
1½ cups shredded low-moisture mozzarella
6 to 12 large leaves fresh basil
Salt and freshly ground black pepper
Sunflower or other high-heat oil for frying
1 cup pecorino

> Make a piña colada, Puerto Rico's national drink, for the Sharks, and a Manhattan for the Jets.

TO MAKE THE DOUGH

1. Sift the flour, baking powder, and salt into a large bowl.

2. Cut the shortening into the flour, using a pastry cutter or a fork.

3. Incorporate the egg into the mixture.

4. Add the water a little at a time, mixing until the dough is shaggy. Press the dough together and transfer to a floured work surface. Knead for 3 to 5 minutes, until smooth and pliable. Form into a ball, cover with plastic wrap, and let rest for at least 30 minutes. The dough can be made ahead of time and refrigerated for up to 2 days.

5. Divide the dough into 12 equal pieces. Form each piece into a ball and use a rolling pin to roll out into ⅛-inch-thick rounds.

TO MAKE THE FILLING

1. Combine the minced garlic and the olive oil in a small skillet. Heat until the garlic just starts to sizzle, then transfer to a heatproof bowl and add the parsley.

2. Slice the fresh mozzarella into ¼-inch-thick half-moons.

3. Spoon a small amount of the pizza sauce into one-half of a dough round and top with both kinds of mozzarella. Tear one to two large basil leaves on top of the cheese and season with salt and pepper. Take care not to overfill.

4. Fold the round in half and crimp the edges with a fork. Repeat with the other dough rounds.

5. Fill a Dutch oven or large pot with 2 inches of frying oil. Heat to 350°F and fry the empanadillas in batches until they are golden brown and crispy, flipping halfway through.

6. Transfer to a paper towel to drain. Allow to cool briefly before brushing or drizzling with the parsley mixture and sprinkling liberally with the pecorino.

CONTINUED ▶

The opening scenes were filmed on West 68th Street between Amsterdam and West End Avenues in buildings that were about to be demolished as part of the Lincoln Center urban renewal project.

SAL'S FAMOUS PIZZA

DO THE RIGHT THING (1989)

MOZZARELLA, MARINARA, THIN CRUST

YIELD: 3 PIZZAS
ALLERGIES: DAIRY, GLUTEN
TOOLS: PIZZA STONE, PIZZA PADDLE

A classic New York–style pizza just as Sal would have served. Extra cheese is $2.

FOR THE DOUGH

1¼ cups 100°F water
2 teaspoons yeast
1 tablespoon kosher salt
1½ tablespoons sugar
4 cups all-purpose flour
3 tablespoons olive oil, plus more for pan

FOR THE SAUCE

One 28-ounce can crushed tomatoes
1 tablespoon minced garlic (from about 3 cloves)
3 tablespoons dried oregano
1 teaspoon freshly ground black pepper
2 teaspoons salt
3 tablespoons olive oil

FOR ASSEMBLY

¼ cup fine cornmeal
3 medium balls fresh mozzarella, sliced

> New York pizza was first served by Gennaro Lombardi in a grocery store on Spring Street in Manhattan in 1905.

TO MAKE THE DOUGH

1. Mix together the warm water and yeast in a small bowl. Allow to bloom.
2. In a stand mixer fitted with the dough hook (alternatively, this can be kneaded by hand), mix together the salt, sugar, and flour.
3. While mixing on medium speed, add the yeast mixture and oil.
4. Knead for 7 minutes.
5. Divide the dough into thirds. Roll each portion into a ball and place on an oiled pan. Loosely cover with plastic wrap and refrigerate overnight or up to 3 days.
6. Remove from the refrigerator 2 hours before ready to use.

TO MAKE THE SAUCE

1. Mix together all the sauce ingredients in a large bowl.
2. The longer you can let it sit, the richer the flavor will be.

TO ASSEMBLE

1. Preheat the oven to 500°F with a pizza stone on the bottom rack at least 30 minutes before ready to bake.
2. Generously spread the cornmeal on a pizza paddle.
3. Stretch a ball of dough on a floured work surface, press into a 12-inch circle, and place on top of the prepared pizza paddle.
4. Spread the pizza sauce on the dough, starting in the middle and leaving the ½-inch outer margin of crust bare.
5. Top with fresh mozzarella and slide onto the hot pizza stone.
6. Bake for 5 minutes, or until the crust is golden brown and the cheese is bubbling.
7. Serve on paper plates and eat it folded down the middle in proper NYC fashion.

CONTINUED ▶

FM 108 We Love Radio (Samuel L. Jackson, DJ) was inspired by a real radio station Spike Lee saw in Washington, DC, with a window to the street.

STAY PUFTED! | *GHOSTBUSTERS* (1984)

RUM, BLENDED SCOTCH, CRÈME DE CACAO, CINNAMON-FLAVORED WHISKEY, MARSHMALLOW, MOLE BITTERS, STOUT, S'MORE

YIELD: 1 SERVING
ALLERGIES: DAIRY, GLUTEN
GLASSWARE: ROCKS GLASS
TOOL: BLOWTORCH

When a god asks you what form the destructor should take, make sure to not think of *anything*. Even if it's as innocent as fond summer nights out on Camp Waconda, with a s'more in hand.

1.5 ounces aged rum (El Dorado 12-year preferred)

0.375 ounce blended Scotch (Dewar's 12-year preferred)

0.375 ounce crème de cacao (Tempus Fugit preferred)

0.33 ounce cinnamon-flavored whiskey

1 ounce Marshmallow Milk (recipe follows)

1 dash mole or Aztec bitters

Full-bodied stout (Brooklyn Brewery Blackout preferred) for topping

Freshly toasted s'more for garnish

1. Combine the rum, Scotch, crème de cacao, cinnamon-flavored whiskey, Marshmallow Milk, and bitters in a mixing tin, add ice, and shake as if roasting s'mores after a day spent at Camp Waconda.

2. Strain over a rocks glass with fresh ice and top with the stout.

3. Garnish with the freshly toasted s'more.

TO MAKE S'MORES

First, you take the graham. You stick the chocolate on the graham. Then you roast the mallow. When the mallow's flaming, you stick it on the chocolate. Then you cover it with another graham. (Sage advice and guaranteed to work perfectly over either campfire or stovetop.)

CONTINUED ▶

MARSHMALLOW MILK YIELD: 40 TO 50 SERVINGS

**One 12-ounce bag
marshmallows (make sure
they are NOT minis)**

1½ quarts whole milk

1. Separate the marshmallows into two equal portions in a large, shallow baking pan.

2. On one of the sides, take the blowtorch and rain down fire and brimstone (carefully, with proper adult supervision, of course). You want to see black-I-left-it-too-long-in-the-campfire torch marks on the marshmallows.

3. On the other side, toast with the blowtorch until brown, not black. Make sure you are rotating the marshmallows to allow for an even toasting on all sides.

4. Next, transfer the mallows to a large pot, add the milk, and heat over high heat for about 10 minutes. Take care to keep eyes on the milk; the amount of sugar from the marshmallows might cause the milk to froth over if you are not careful.

5. When most of the mallows are dissolved into the milk, remove from the heat and pour through a fine strainer into a heatproof container; label and date.

THIS MAGNIFICENT MEAL

GHOSTBUSTERS (1984)

KUNG PAO CAULIFLOWER, PEANUTS, CHILES DE ÁRBOL

YIELD: 4 TO 6 SERVINGS
ALLERGIES: PEANUTS, SOY
TOOLS: 8-QUART DUTCH OVEN, CANDY THERMOMETER

At the old firehouse headquarters, the three Ghostbusters lift their cans and cheer getting their first (and only) customer. Venkman wants to draw some petty cash to wine and dine their customer, Dana. Motioning to the Chinese takeout before them, Ray replies, "Uhhh . . . this magnificent feast here represents the LAST of the petty cash," to which Venkman responds, "Slow down. Chew your food." Enjoy this vegan re-creation of an American Chinese restaurant staple.

FOR THE SAUCE

2 tablespoons sesame oil
¼ cup minced fresh ginger
2 tablespoons minced garlic
3 scallions, sliced thinly
1 cup soy sauce
½ cup ketchup
¼ cup rice vinegar
¼ cup Shaoxing wine
1 ounce dried chiles de árbol
½ cup water
¼ cup cornstarch

FOR THE CAULIFLOWER

2 heads cauliflower, broken into bite-size florets
3 tablespoons egg replacer (I like Bob's Red Mill)
6 tablespoons water
1 pound white rice flour

FOR FRYING

3 quarts canola or vegetable oil

FOR SERVING

Toasted peanuts
Thinly sliced scallions
Chiles de árbol

TO MAKE THE SAUCE

1. Heat the sesame oil in a 3-quart saucepot until hot but not smoking. Add the ginger, garlic, and scallions and cook until translucent.

2. Add the soy sauce, ketchup, rice vinegar, Shaoxing wine, and chiles de árbol. Whisk to combine and bring to a boil. Combine the water and cornstarch in a small bowl to make a slurry and set aside.

3. Once the sauce has come to a boil, lower the heat to low. Slowly whisk in the cornstarch slurry until the sauce thickens and coats the back of a spoon. Remove from the heat and set aside.

TO MAKE THE CAULIFLOWER

1. Bring heavily salted water to a boil in a large pot and blanch the cauliflower just to take the rawness out of it. Remove from the pot and let the cauliflower cool completely.

2. While the cauliflower is cooling, combine the egg replacer and water in a small bowl and let thicken.

3. Once the cauliflower has cooled completely, toss in half of the rice flour until completely coated.

4. Toss the coated cauliflower in the thickened egg replacer and then toss the cauliflower in the remaining rice flour a second time, until completely coated.

CONTINUED ▶

The traditional Szech-uan version of this dish is named after the governor of the Szechuan province during the Qing dynasty. The name is a pun, as the Chinese character can also mean "little cube" and mirrors the cubes the chicken is cut into.

TO FRY

1. Heat the canola oil to 350°F in an 8-quart Dutch oven over medium heat; use a candy thermometer to check the temperature.

2. Fry the coated cauliflower in batches until golden brown, keeping the heat as close to 350°F as possible.

3. Toss the fried cauliflower in the sauce.

4. Serve with toasted peanuts, thinly sliced scallions, and more chiles de árbol.

The marketing campaign for *Ghostbusters* began in the spring of 1984, when pin-back buttons were handed out on the street and billboards were posted featuring just the logo with no type or any clue as to what was being promoted.

OUR PASTA THIS EVENING

AMERICAN PSYCHO (2000)

SQUID INK RICOTTA RAVIOLI, LEMONGRASS BROTH

YIELD: 2 SERVINGS
ALLERGIES: DAIRY, FISH, GLUTEN, SHELLFISH
TOOL: PASTRY CUTTER OR RAVIOLI CUTTER

A direct quote from the opening sequence, which takes place in a restaurant with overly ornate food. As the intro credits appear on-screen, a server is explaining the night's special to the guests.

FOR THE RAVIOLI

1 cup ricotta

2 tablespoons squid ink

2 tablespoon chopped fresh chives

1 teaspoon lemon zest

1 teaspoon salt

¼ teaspoon freshly ground black pepper

2 sheets prepared pasta

1 large egg, whisked

FOR THE BROTH

1 tablespoon unsalted butter

1 tablespoon all-purpose flour

2 cups fish stock

¼ cup peeled and sliced lemongrass

1 garlic clove, sliced

1 tablespoon julienned fresh ginger

Freshly ground black pepper for garnish

TO MAKE THE RAVIOLI

1. Combine the ricotta, squid ink, chives, lemon zest, salt, and pepper in a bowl and mix together until consistent.

2. Transfer the mixture to a pastry bag or resealable plastic bag with a ½-inch hole cut into the bottom (or lower corner, if using a plastic bag).

3. Roll out a sheet of pasta until as thin as cardboard.

4. Pipe a tablespoon of filling onto the pasta, leaving a 1-inch bare margin all the way around the edge.

5. Roll out the other sheet of pasta to the same thickness.

6. Wet your fingers with the beaten egg and wet the bottom layer of pasta all around the filling and to the edges.

7. Place the second sheet of pasta on top, layering it from one end to the other, trying to allow as much air out from around the filling as possible.

8. Press all edges to seal.

9. Cut out the ravioli with a pastry cutter or ravioli cutter.

10. Bring 2 quarts of salted water to a rolling boil in a large pot.

11. Drop in the ravioli and cook until al dente.

12. Remove from the pot and set aside.

CONTINUED ▶

Lemongrass (*Cymbopogon citratus*) is a tall, perennial grass in a class of about 45 species of grasses native to the tropical and subtropical climates of Asia, Australia, and Africa.

TO MAKE THE BROTH

1. Melt the butter in a large skillet.
2. Whisk in the flour until incorporated.
3. Slowly add the fish stock while whisking.
4. Add the lemongrass, garlic, and ginger.
5. Bring to a simmer and simmer for 5 minutes.
6. Place the ravioli in the sauce and allow them to become coated with the sauce for 2 minutes.
7. Remove from the heat and spoon the ravioli into bowls.
8. Top with the sauce.
9. Garnish with freshly ground black pepper.

The majority of *American Psycho*'s budget was used to license the '80s pop soundtrack.

THE SHOULDER TOUCH

SPIDER-MAN: INTO THE SPIDER-VERSE (2018)

RUM, RASPBERRY, HOUSE-MADE SAZÓN, AVERNA

YIELD: 1 SERVING
GLASSWARE: CHILLED ROCKS GLASS

Miles Morales's origin story is a fresh take on the Spider-Man franchise. Bacardi 8-Year and a Sazón-spiced honey syrup combine to create a smooth libation you can sip on during this action-packed film. One of our favorites of the past decade.

- 1.5 ounces Bacardi Reserva Ocho 8-Year Rum
- 0.5 ounce St. George Raspberry Liqueur
- 0.25 ounce House-Made Sazón-Spiced Honey Syrup (recipe follows)
- 0.33 ounce Amaro Averna
- Skewer of blackberries and raspberries, predusted in Mock Sazón, for garnish

1. Combine the Bacardi, St. George Raspberry, spiced syrup, and Amaro Averna in a mixing glass, add ice, and stir until diluted and chilled.

2. Strain into a chilled rocks glass without ice.

3. Garnish with the skewer of Sazón-dusted blackberries and raspberries.

CONTINUED ▶

TO BE CONTINUED...

HOUSE-MADE SAZÓN–SPICED HONEY SYRUP

YIELD: 15 TO 20 SERVINGS

1 tablespoon ground coriander

1 tablespoon ground cumin

1 tablespoon ground
  annatto seeds

1 tablespoon garlic powder

2 teaspoons dried oregano

1 teaspoon onion powder

2 cups honey

1 cup water

Stan Lee is pictured in every train that goes by.

1. First, combine all the dry ingredients in a bowl and mix thoroughly to incorporate. This creates your own Sazón-style seasoning.

2. Then, combine the honey and water in a pot and bring to a boil.

3. Add approximately half of the Sazón seasoning you've prepared and simmer over medium-low heat for 5 minutes. Reserve the rest of the Sazón for other uses, including to dust the garnish.

4. Allow the syrup to cool, then strain the syrup through a fine strainer, label, and date.

Lactic acid is a naturally occurring organic compound found in many foods, especially dairy products. It is a common additive in some styles of beer and can be purchased in liquid form from brewing supply stores.

ADVENTURELAND STASH

GOOD TIME (2017)

VODKA, CUCUMBER LEMONGRASS SHRUB, SPRITE, LACTIC ACID

YIELD: 1 SERVING
ALLERGY: LACTIC ACID
(SEE NOTE ON OPPOSITE PAGE)
GLASSWARE: 8-OUNCE GLASS
SPRITE BOTTLE

This drink is a reimagining of the Sprite bottle that is spiked with LSD in the film. We add two types of acid: lactic and acetic (vinegar). The name refers to the amusement park where the LSD is stashed.

1.5 ounces vodka

0.75 ounce Cucumber
Shrub (recipe follows)

1 dropperful (about 1 ml)
lactic acid

One 8-ounce bottle of Sprite

1. Combine the vodka, shrub, and lactic acid in a food-grade plastic container and chill in the freezer for at least 20 minutes.

2. Open the Sprite bottle and pour out all but 3 ounces. (You can enjoy the rest of the Sprite separately.)

3. Add the chilled ingredients to the 3 ounces of Sprite in the bottle.

CUCUMBER SHRUB

1 cup white vinegar

2 cups chopped cucumber

1 cup sugar

1. Bring the vinegar to a light boil in a nonreactive saucepot.

2. Combine the cucumber and sugar in a blender.

3. Top with the hot vinegar and blend until the sugar is dissolved.

4. Strain and refrigerate.

This character of Caliph is played by Brooklyn-born rapper Necro, who had previously worked with the Safdie brothers in *Heaven Knows What* (2014).

Based on the Brooklyn cocktail, it is one of five cocktails named for the boroughs of New York City, along with the Bronx, the Manhattan, the Queens, and the Staten Island Ferry. It resembles a Manhattan but with a specific type of bitters (several types of bitters can be used in a Manhattan) and the addition of Maraschino liqueur. It largely fell into obscurity after the end of Prohibition but experienced a resurgence in the 1990s.

ANYBODY WANT A MILKSHAKE?

THE FRENCH CONNECTION (1971)

COGNAC, BLANC VERMOUTH, CRÈME DE CASSIS, AMER PICON

YIELD: 1 SERVING
GLASSWARE: COUPE GLASS

The film is set in Brooklyn, so this is a variation of a Brooklyn cocktail, but it substitutes the ingredients for French versions as a nod to the French connection, the origin of the drugs and the antagonist in the film. The name is a reference to a scene in which Popeye Doyle makes a "milkshake" using discarded drugs from the bar patrons that he is shaking down for information.

2 ounces cognac
1 ounce French blanc vermouth
  (such as Dolin Blanc or Lillet)
0.25 ounce Amer Picon
0.25 ounce crème de cassis
Lemon peel for garnish

1. Combine all the ingredients, except the garnish, in an ice-filled cocktail shaking tin.
2. Shake and strain into a chilled coupe glass.
3. Garnish with the lemon peel.

The scene where Popeye Doyle busts the bar and makes the "Milk Shake" with the discarded narcotics is located at 1128 Myrtle Avenue in Brooklyn and is now a Popeyes Chicken–founded by Arthur Copland, who actually named his chain of restaurants after the Popeye Doyle character.

AUDREY II | *LITTLE SHOP OF HORRORS* (1986)

RYE WHISKEY, BEET-INFUSED SWEET VERMOUTH, CYNAR

YIELD: 1 SERVING
GLASSWARE: COUPE GLASS

Named after the carnivorous plant from the film, this drink is a variation on the Manhattan cocktail, a nod to the setting, with the addition of some vegetal ingredients: Cynar (an artichoke-based herbal liqueur), resembling the plant monster, and beets, resembling the blood that it drinks.

1.5 ounces rye whiskey

1 ounce Beet-Infused Sweet Vermouth (recipe follows)

0.5 ounce Cynar

Lemon peel for garnish

1. Combine all the ingredients, except the lemon peel, in an ice-filled mixing glass.

2. Stir and strain into a chilled coupe.

3. Garnish with the lemon peel.

BEET-INFUSED SWEET VERMOUTH

One 750-milliliter bottle sweet vermouth

1 cup washed and chopped beet (no need to peel)

1. Combine the sweet vermouth with the beets in a food-safe jar or plastic container.

2. Let sit for 24 hours, then strain.

Made in the pre-CGI era, the plant "Audrey II" required up to 60 technicians to operate. Brian Henson, son of Muppets creator Jim Henson, was one of the puppeteers.

BOOZE & BOOKS:

FILMS ADAPTED
FROM BOOKS

Booze & Books combines three of our favorite things—books, movies, and cocktails—and films adapted from books are the perfect way to celebrate the relationship between two of culture's most beloved mediums. Since the start of cinema, books have provided the road map for filmmakers, and in return, cinema-lovers have gotten Mary Shelley's *Frankenstein* turning into James Whale's *Frankenstein* (1931) and Roald Dahl's *Charlie and the Chocolate Factory* giving us Gene Wilder as the iconic, eccentric candyman in *Willy Wonka & the Chocolate Factory*.

Sometimes it's controversial as to which one is better, and that's a fun argument we encourage, but when done right, few sights are better than seeing your favorite characters and stories come to life on the big screen. Add an inspired drink to that and it's heaven!

TYPE O NEGATIVE

ONLY LOVERS LEFT ALIVE (2013)

RUM, BLOOD ORANGE, POMEGRANATE, LIME, MINT

YIELD: 6 ICE POPS
TOOLS: ICE POP MOLDS AND
WOODEN ICE POP STICKS

While Adam and Eve catch up over a chess match, reminiscing about Mary Wollstonecraft (one of the founding feminist philosophers of the 18th century), whom Adam admits was delicious, Eve shares a tasty O negative blood ice pop treat with him.

½ **cup water**

½ **cup sugar**

1 **ounce fresh mint**

16 **ounces fresh blood
    orange juice**

4 **ounces pomegranate juice**

1 **ounce fresh lime juice**

4 **ounces white rum**

1. Bring the water and sugar to a boil in a small saucepan. Remove from the heat and steep the mint for 10 minutes while the simple syrup cools. Strain out the mint leaves.

2. Once the mint-flavored syrup has cooled, combine the blood orange, pomegranate, and lime juice with the rum and syrup.

3. Pour the liquid into an ice pop mold, leaving about ¼ inch of headspace for the liquid to expand.

4. Place the ice pop sticks into the individual molds and freeze for a minimum of 3 hours.

While technically named after the Dave Wallis science fiction novel of the same name from 1964 (hence the placement in our Booze & Books chapter), the plots have no similarities. A film adaptation was planned in the mid-1960s for director Nicholas Ray (a picture of him can later be seen in the movie) starring the Rolling Stones. What might have been . . .

TYERSALL PARK | *CRAZY RICH ASIANS (2018)*

GIN, POMELO, CUCUMBER, FLEUR DE SEL, SPARKLING MINERAL WATER

YIELD: 1 SERVING
GLASSWARE: COLLINS GLASS
TOOL: MANDOLINE

Arriving at Tyersall Park from the other side of the world might feel a little daunting, especially when everyone around you is speaking Cantonese, not Mandarin! At least you'll find solace in this Southeast Asian riff on a Salty Dog.

---

1 English cucumber

Lime wedge for rimming glass

Fleur de sel for rimming glass

1.5 ounces The Botanist Islay Dry Gin

1 heavy barspoon Rich Simple Syrup (recipe follows)

1 heavy barspoon fresh lime juice

4 ounces fresh pomelo juice

Topo Chico to top

1. Carefully cut the cucumber lengthwise with a sharp knife to create a straight and level base.

2. Adjust your mandoline to the thinnest setting and slice the cucumber, flesh side down, across the mandoline to create a thin cucumber slice.

3. Run a lime wedge along half the rim of the collins glass to create an adhesive. Place some fleur de sel in a saucer and dip the rim of the glass into it.

4. In a spiraling motion, arrange your cucumber slice inside the collins glass until it reaches the rim of the glass.

5. Build all of the liquid ingredients in order in the collins glass, ending with the Topo Chico. Add ice and serve immediately.

RICH SIMPLE SYRUP   **YIELD:** 10 TO 12 SERVINGS

1¾ cups sugar

½ cup water

1. Combine the sugar and water in a pot, bring to a boil, and boil for 5 minutes.

2. Turn off the heat, allow to cool, then bottle and refrigerate.

CONTINUED ▶

The pomelo (*Citrus maxima* or *Citrus grandis*) is a natural citrus fruit native to Southeast Asia. It is the largest citrus fruit from the family Rutaceae and the principal ancestor of the grapefruit.

In *Crazy Rich Asians*, the scene where Astrid Young Teo, played by Gemma Chan, is introduced was shot at the Astor Bar inside the St. Regis Kuala Lumpur. The bartenders have since created a cocktail called the Astrid, consisting of Jose Cuervo silver tequila, pomegranate juice, lemon bitters, and elderflower foam.

OLD-FASHIONED JUSTICE

IF BEALE STREET COULD TALK (2018)

WHISKEY, DEMERARA SYRUP, BITTERS, ORANGE PEEL

YIELD: 1 SERVING
GLASSWARE: ROCKS GLASS

The plot centers on Fonny, a man wrongly committed for raping a Puerto Rican woman in NYC and the effect this injustice has on Tish, the soon-to-be mother of his son Alonzo Jr. This old fashioned cocktail uses Uncle Nearest whiskey—a relatively new brand whose name pays homage to a slave named Nathan "Nearest" Green, one of the original pillars of the Tennessee bourbon community. Only in the last five years has Jack Daniel's publicly credited this man for developing the company's original whiskey recipe and mentoring Jack Daniel in the ways of distilling.

"Not everything that is faced can be changed, but nothing can be changed until it is faced." —James Baldwin, *The Cross of Redemption: Uncollected Writings* (2010)

---

2 ounces Uncle Nearest 1856 premium aged whiskey

1 demerara sugar cube

1 heavy barspoon Demerara Syrup (recipe follows)

3 dashes Angostura Bitters

Orange peel

1. Combine the whiskey, sugar cube, and demerara syrup in a mixing glass and, with a muddler, break the sugar cube until the sugar has dissolved.
2. Add the bitters and ice, and stir for 20 to 30 seconds, until diluted.
3. Strain into a chilled rocks glass with fresh ice.
4. Garnish with the orange peel and serve immediately.

DEMERARA SYRUP   YIELD: ½ CUP

1¾ cups demerara sugar

½ cup water

1. Combine the demerara sugar and water in a pot and bring to a boil, stirring occasionally.
2. Once fully incorporated, pour into a bottle and refrigerate.

CONTINUED ▶

Uncle Nearest is rewriting whiskey's history to include people of color and women, and expanding Tennessee whiskey's identity far beyond its role as the liquid logo for the old boys' club. The brand sponsors every one of Nearest Green's descendants to go through schooling—as long as they keep their grades above a 3.0.

Director Barry Jenkins and cinematographer James Laxton took inspiration from photographer Roy DeCarava's work for lighting and composition; DeCarava is originally from NYC's Harlem, where the story is set.

MOLOKO PLUS | *A CLOCKWORK ORANGE* (1971)

VODKA, MEZCAL, YELLOW CHARTREUSE, ANCHO CHILE, BANANA MILK, LEMON

YIELD: 1 SERVING
ALLERGY: DAIRY
GLASSWARE: COLLINS GLASS

Served at the Korova Milk Bar in the film, Moloko Plus is milk plus the addition of several "veshches" (drugs). This boozy milk is spiked with some of our favorite flavors.

1 ounce vodka
0.25 ounce mezcal
0.75 ounce Yellow Chartreuse
0.5 ounce ancho chile liqueur
0.25 ounce fresh lemon juice
0.25 ounce simple syrup
2 ounces milk
½ overripe banana
Nutmeg

1. Blend together all the ingredients, except the nutmeg, in a blender.

2. Strain into an ice-filled collins glass.

3. Grate fresh nutmeg on top.

ULTRA-VIOLENCE |

A CLOCKWORK ORANGE (1971)

RYE WHISKEY, BLOOD ORANGE FIVE-SPICE SHRUB, CIOCIARO, BITTERS

YIELD: 1 SERVING
GLASSWARE: ROCKS GLASS

This filly of a firegold will open your glazz(es) to what a little sakar and spice can do to an "Ultra-Violence" Sazerac. Vareet the firegold for ya droogs, correct your otchkies, and enjoy Kubrick's simmy.

2 ounces Rittenhouse
  Straight Rye Whiskey

0.25 ounce Amaro CioCiaro

0.5 ounce Blood Orange Five-
  Spice Shrub (recipe follows)

2 dashes Peychaud's Bitters

1 cinnamon stick

2-inch square ice cube

Bloodshot eyeball
  candy for garnish

1. Add the rye, amaro, shrub, and bitters to your mixing glass, add ice, and stir for 10 to 15 seconds.

2. Take the cinnamon stick and light on fire with a match, then cover it with the rocks glass for 5 seconds to imbue the glass with smoke.

3. Place the square ice cube in the smoked rocks glass and strain the cocktail into the glass.

4. Garnish with the bloodshot candy eyeball.

BLOOD ORANGE FIVE-SPICE SHRUB   YIELD: 18 TO 22 SERVINGS

4 star anise

5 cinnamon sticks

10 whole cardamom pods

10 whole cloves

10 black peppercorns

4 cups sugar

1 quart champagne vinegar

¾ cup + 1½ tablespoons honey

2 cups blood orange
  concentrate

1. Place the star anise, cinnamon sticks, cardamom, cloves, and peppercorns in a cold, dry skillet and toast over medium-high heat until the aromatics are released, 3 to 5 minutes. Remove from the heat.

2. Combine the sugar, vinegar, honey, and toasted spices in a large, nonreactive pot, bring to a light boil, and boil for 10 minutes.

3. Lower the heat to a simmer and add the blood orange concentrate. Cook, stirring occasionally, for another 5 minutes.

4. Remove from the heat, allow the shrub to cool, then strain out the spices, label, and date.

The older writer's assistant is played by former bodybuilder David Prowse, who went on to play Darth Vader in the *Star Wars* films.

ROSEMARY'S BABY

ROSEMARY'S BABY (1968)

BOURBON, RED WINE, AMARO, ROSEMARY SYRUP, LEMON, BITTERS

YIELD: 1 SERVING
GLASSWARE: COLLINS GLASS

This variation on a New York Sour is a nod to the setting of the film, and the blood red wine float gives the drink an appropriately ominous appearance.

1 ounce bourbon
1.25 ounces red wine
0.75 ounce amaro
0.75 ounce fresh lemon juice
0.75 ounce Rosemary
  Syrup (recipe follows)
2 dashes Angostura Bitters
1 sprig rosemary for garnish

1. Combine all the ingredients, except the rosemary, in an ice-filled cocktail shaking tin.
2. Shake and strain into an ice-filled, chilled collins glass.
3. Garnish with the sprig of rosemary.

ROSEMARY SYRUP

1 cup + 3 tablespoons sugar
1 cup water
¼ cup fresh rosemary leaves
3 tablespoons whole
  black peppercorns
Peel of 1 lemon

1. Combine the sugar and water in a pot and bring to a boil.
2. Add the rosemary and peppercorns and simmer over low heat for 15 minutes. Add the lemon peel and simmer for an additional 5 minutes.
3. Remove from the heat and leave the aromatics in while the syrup cools. Once cool, strain and refrigerate.

The film was shot in the famous Dakota apartment house near Central Park, former home to Boris Karloff, Lauren Bacall, Jack Palance, and John Lennon, among others.

WE'RE GONNA NEED A BIGGER BOAT | *JAWS (1975)*

LOBSTER, MEYER LEMON, TARRAGON, SWEET HAWAIIAN BUN

YIELD: 4 SERVINGS
ALLERGIES: DAIRY, EGGS, GLUTEN, SHELLFISH, SOY

While you watch the ocean make a meal out of us on-screen, take some solace from making a meal out of the ocean off-screen with this Northeast classic of hunks of lobster meat seasoned simply and piled high on a pillowy roll.

Note: If you can't find the King's Hawaiian, you can substitute brioche or another long bun with a little bit of sweetness.

- **3 small lobsters, or 2 pounds lobster meat**
- **½ red onion, diced**
- **Zest and juice of 1 Meyer lemon**
- **¾ cup mayonnaise**
- **1 teaspoon finely chopped fresh tarragon**
- **¾ cup small-diced celery, tender inner leaves included**
- **Salt and freshly ground black pepper**
- **One 12-ounce package King's Original Sweet Hawaiian Hot Dog Buns (see note)**
- **1 tablespoon finely chopped fresh chives (optional)**

1. If not using whole lobsters, skip to step 3. Select a pot enough to fit all three lobsters, fill with water, and bring to a boil. Cook the lobsters for 12 to 15 minutes depending on size.

2. Remove the lobsters from the pot. Crack and remove the meat, making sure to check for any stray shells. Chop or tear into pieces slightly larger than bite-size.

3. Place the red onion in a nonreactive bowl and cover with ice water. Allow to sit for 20 minutes, then rinse and drain.

4. Combine the Meyer lemon juice, ¼ teaspoon of the zest, and the mayonnaise, tarragon, red onion, and celery in a large, nonreactive bowl and mix well.

5. Fold in the lobster meat and season to taste with salt and pepper.

6. Spoon the salad into buns and garnish with the chives, if using.

Bruce, the mechanical shark, was frequently impossible to operate due to ocean water infiltrating and corroding the pneumatic hoses that controlled it. This potential disaster forced the 26-year-old director, Steven Spielberg, to only use the mechanical shark in the later scenes of Jaws, and creatively suggest the presence of the shark in the early scenes of the film, creating a more tense and suspenseful film overall.

TRY THE VEAL, IT'S THE BEST IN THE CITY | *THE GODFATHER* (1972)

VEAL SCALOPPINE, SUN-DRIED TOMATOES, OLIVES, BLOOD ORANGE, NEW POTATOES

YIELD: 4 SERVINGS
ALLERGIES: DAIRY, GLUTEN
TOOL: MALLET

The Godfather movie trilogy has an interesting relationship with oranges. In every scene where there is a deeply meaningful death, oranges can be seen.

Four 6-ounce veal cutlets, either leg or top round

All-purpose flour for dredging

¼ cup canola or vegetable oil

1 pound new potatoes, sliced into ¼-inch-thick slices

1 cup low-sodium chicken stock

1 cup Nyon or Kalamata olives, drained, rinsed, halved, and pitted

1 cup jarred sun-dried tomatoes, drained and cut into strips

3 sprigs thyme

1 blood orange, sliced into ⅛-inch-thick rings

Salt and freshly ground black pepper

4 tablespoons (½ stick) unsalted butter

1. Lay the cutlets between two pieces of plastic wrap and gently pound, using a mallet, until roughly ¼ inch thick. Dredge the veal in flour, making sure that the veal is covered entirely but there is no excess flour.

2. Heat the oil in a large sauté pan over medium-high heat until shimmering. Gently lay the dredged veal into the hot oil, lower the heat to medium, and cook until first side is golden brown. Flip the veal to the second side.

3. Once you have flipped the veal, add the potatoes and chicken stock. Bring the stock to a simmer and cook until the potatoes are tender.

4. Add the olives, sun-dried tomatoes, thyme sprigs, and blood orange rings. Season with salt and pepper.

5. Remove the cooked veal and potatoes from the stock and serve on a large serving platter. Whisk the butter into the pan juices to create a sauce and pour over top of the veal and potatoes.

The name of this recipe is based on the line uttered by Captain McCluskey when Michael comes back from the bathroom with the gun. The scene is set on Arthur Avenue in the Bronx, the less-traveled home for Italian Americans and the restaurants that grew up around where they settled in the city.

Oranges appear seven different times in *The Godfather* alone and more frequently in the sequels. The symbolism has been a source of debate for decades.

GREASER'S SANDWICH

THE OUTSIDERS (1983)

COLA BBQ PULLED CHICKEN, SLAW, POTATO BUN

YIELD: 4 SERVINGS
ALLERGY: GLUTEN (CHECK POTATO BUN LABEL FOR DAIRY OR SOY; CHECK MAYO FOR SOY)

While Ponyboy and Johnny are on the lam, they have to eat bread and bologna, so when Dally comes to talk to them, they go get something real to eat: BBQ pulled pork sandwiches from a Dairy Queen drive-through. Classic '60s food.

FOR THE CHICKEN
18 ounces cola
1 cup apple cider vinegar
½ cup tomato paste
¼ cup molasses
1 tablespoon chili powder
1 tablespoon salt
1½ teaspoons freshly ground black pepper
6 chicken thighs
1 tablespoon white vinegar
1 teaspoon cornstarch
1 teaspoon water

FOR THE SLAW
4 cups finely sliced green cabbage
1 cup julienned Granny Smith apple
½ cup julienned carrot
1 teaspoon salt
½ cup mayonnaise
¼ cup apple cider vinegar
2 tablespoons poppy seeds

FOR SERVING
Potato buns

TO MAKE THE CHICKEN

1. Preheat the oven to 300°F.

2. Mix together the cola, vinegar, tomato paste, molasses, chili powder, and salt and black pepper in a roasting pan.

3. Put the chicken into the cola mixture in a single later and cover the pan with foil.

4. Bake for 3 hours, or until the chicken shreds when being pulled.

5. Leaving the sauce in its roasting pan, remove the chicken from the sauce and place on a cutting board.

6. Shred by hand or with two forks while sprinkling with the white vinegar.

7. Place the roasting pan of sauce over very low heat.

8. Mix the cornstarch and water together in a small bowl to turn into slurry, then whisk into the sauce.

9. Cook the sauce until thick, about 10 minutes.

10. Return the chicken to the sauce and mix until well coated.

CONTINUED ▶

Other outsiders that bonded at Dairy Queen: No Doubt band members Eric Stefani and John Spence met while working at the same Dairy Queen in 1986.

TO MAKE THE SLAW

1. Mix together the cabbage, apple, and carrot in a large bowl.
2. Add the salt and mix again.
3. Stir together the mayonnaise, vinegar, and poppy seeds in a small, separate bowl.
4. Add the dressing to the slaw and mix well.

TO ASSEMBLE

1. Place a large scoop of shredded chicken on the bottom half of a potato bun.
2. Top with a large scoop of slaw.
3. Top with the upper bun half.
4. Grab napkins.

S. E. Hinton, who wrote the original novel at age 15, has a cameo as a nurse in the hospital scene with Matt Dillon.

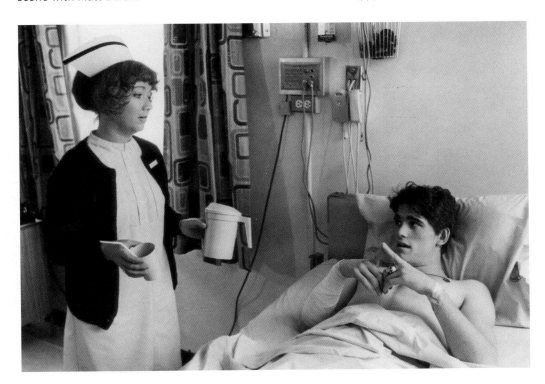

SMOKING HEYWARD | *SCROOGED* (1988)

RUBY PORT, RED WINE, ORANGE, CLOVES, ALLSPICE, NUTMEG OR RUM

YIELD: 12 SERVINGS
GLASSWARE: COCKTAIL MUG

A Smoking Bishop was a popular Christmastime punch in Victorian England. It is referred to directly by Scrooge in *A Christmas Carol*, the source material of the film. The name also references several characters that are smoking or set on fire. The flaming version is a reference to a scene with a Baked Alaska flambéed with rum, and "take it easy on the Bacardi" is a quote from the movie.

2 oranges
12 whole cloves
One 750-milliliter bottle red wine
½ cup demerara sugar
6 allspice berries
1 tablespoon roughly chopped fresh ginger
One 750-milliliter bottle ruby port
Nutmeg for garnish (optional)
Bacardi 151 Rum (optional)

1. Preheat the oven to 350°F.
2. Cut the oranges in half and place flat side down on a baking sheet. Stud the orange halves with the cloves (roughly 6 cloves per half). Bake for 1 hour.
3. Combine the red wine, demerara sugar, allspice berries, ginger, and the cooked oranges in a large, nonreactive pot. Bring almost to a boil, then lower the heat to low and allow to simmer for 30 minutes.
4. Remove from the heat, strain, and add the ruby port.
5. Serve warm with nutmeg freshly grated on top. Alternatively, float a spoonful of Bacardi 151 on top and light on fire, but "take it easy on the Bacardi."

Bill Murray turned down the lead roles in *Rain Man*, *Big*, and *Cocktail* (all also released in 1988) to make this film.

RED RUM | *THE SHINING (1980)*

RUM, HIBISCUS SYRUP, LIME, BITTERS

YIELD: 1 SERVING
GLASSWARE: COUPE GLASS

Murder spelled backward has never tasted so good. You set 'em up, I'll knock 'em back.

2 ounces rum
1 ounce Hibiscus Syrup
  (recipe follows)
1 ounce fresh lime juice
3 dashes Peychaud's Bitters

1. Combine all the ingredients in an ice-filled mixing glass.
2. Stir and strain into a chilled coupe glass.

HIBISCUS SYRUP   YIELD: 1 CUP

1 cup + 3 tablespoons sugar
1 cup water
½ cup dried hibiscus flowers

1. Combine the sugar, water, and hibiscus in a pot and bring to a boil, then lower the heat and simmer for 30 minutes.
2. Remove from the heat and strain.

LLOYD | *THE SHINING* (1980)

BOURBON-BRAISED SHORT RIBS, SWEET POTATO CAKES, BOURBON REDUCTION

YIELD: 4 SERVINGS
ALLERGIES: DAIRY, EGG,
FISH (OR CHOOSE VEGAN
WORCESTERSHIRE), GLUTEN
TOOLS: 5-QUART DUTCH OVEN,
TONGS

Inspired by a classic dish you may have enjoyed in the heyday of the Overlook Hotel. Jack is clearly becoming demented and bellies up to the bar, requesting "the hair of the dog that bit me." Lloyd the bartender replies, "Bourbon on the rocks." It's the beginning of the end, a wild finish to *The Shining*.

FOR THE SHORT RIBS

3 pounds boneless short ribs

Kosher salt and freshly
  ground black pepper

1 tablespoon olive oil

1 yellow onion, diced

4 garlic cloves, minced

¾ cup bourbon

½ cup pure maple syrup

2½ cups beef or
  vegetable stock

1 tablespoon minced
  fresh rosemary

2 tablespoons tomato paste

1 tablespoon
  Worcestershire sauce

FOR THE GLAZE (OPTIONAL)

⅔ cup pure maple syrup

2 tablespoons
  Worcestershire sauce

Kosher salt and freshly
  ground black pepper

FOR THE SWEET POTATO CAKES

1½ pounds sweet potatoes

⅓ cup diced green onion

1 tablespoon minced
  fresh cilantro

2 tablespoons sour cream

1 large egg

½ cup plain bread crumbs

1 large garlic clove, grated

Salt and freshly ground
  black pepper

Canola oil for cooking

TO MAKE THE SHORT RIBS

1. Preheat the oven to 325°F.

2. Pat the short ribs dry and season them generously with salt and pepper. Heat the olive oil in a 5-quart Dutch oven over medium-high heat. Working in batches, add the short ribs and sear until browned on all sides, 4 to 5 minutes per side. Transfer to a plate.

3. Lower the heat to medium and let the Dutch oven cool (about 5 minutes), leaving all the oil and drippings in the pan. Add the onion and cook, stirring occasionally, until softened, about 8 minutes. Add the garlic and cook, stirring occasionally, until fragrant, about 1 minute.

4. Add the bourbon and maple syrup and cook until reduced by half, 3 to 4 minutes. Stir in the stock, rosemary, tomato paste, and Worcestershire sauce. Nestle the short ribs in the sauce. The ribs should be almost completely covered with liquid; if necessary, add a little more stock or water (up to about ½ cup) to cover the ribs.

5. Increase the heat to medium-high and bring to a boil. Cover, transfer to the oven, and bake, stirring every 45 minutes, until the ribs are very tender, 2 to 3 hours. Transfer the ribs to a serving platter, cover loosely with aluminum foil, and let them rest for at least 10 minutes.

TO MAKE THE GLAZE (IF USING)

1. Combine the maple syrup and Worcestershire sauce in a small saucepan over high heat and bring to a boil. Cook, stirring, until reduced to a thick glaze, about 5 minutes. Season with salt and pepper.

2. Uncover the ribs. There may be some congealed fat on top of the ribs, which can be scooped off before serving. Divvy the ribs among plates and drizzle the glaze, if using, over the ribs. Serve right away.

TO MAKE THE SWEET POTATO CAKES

1. Preheat the oven to 350°F. Wash the sweet potatoes well, poke a couple of holes in them with a knife, wrap in foil, and bake until soft. The bake time will depend on how large your sweet potatoes are. If you get smaller ones, you can significantly decrease cooking time. Once done, remove from the oven and let cool until easy to handle. Scoop out all the potato meat into a large bowl.

2. Mash the sweet potatoes until smooth.

3. Add the green onions, cilantro, sour cream, egg, bread crumbs, and garlic and mix well.

4. Add salt and pepper, mix well, and taste to make sure you have added enough.

5. Heat a medium sauté pan over medium heat. Add ½ cup of canola oil.

6. Form the sweet potato mixture into patties (about 3 ounces each) and cook for 5 to 7 minutes on each side, until golden brown, using a small spatula to flip carefully.

Jack Nicholson, a former volunteer fireman, was keen to use his door-axing skills in the iconic "Here's Johnny" scene.

MUSIC DRIVEN:

MUSIC SEEN THROUGH FILM

This chapter presents documentaries, performance films, and sometimes just a movie with a killer soundtrack, all united by the common thread of music of all kinds—coinciding with a new golden age in music documentaries produced and released by their own filmmakers, often touring cinemas with their work themselves, much the way independent bands have traditionally done. Whereby at one time being too specialized with your subject matter was a hindrance, the last decade has shown that there are substantial audiences who will come out to theatrical screenings.

With such guests as TV on the Radio, Todd Phillips, Vivien Goldman, Ralph McDaniels, JD Samson, Henry Chalfant, Darryl Jenifer, Penelope Spheeris, Charlie Ahearn, Jerry Harrison, Guy Picciotto, Jem Cohen, JG Thirwell, Sharon Jones, Charles Bradley, and many others, Nitehawk has been very fortunate to connect these musicians and filmmakers in person with a passionate and supportive audience at our event screenings and Q&A appearances.

HAVE A COLA AND SMILE

SORRY TO BOTHER YOU (2018)

WHISKEY, POBLANO CHILE, WALNUT, CHOCOLATE MOLE BITTERS, COLA

YIELD: 1 SERVING
ALLERGY: TREE NUTS (WALNUT)
GLASSWARE: COLLINS GLASS

A theme throughout the movie is the ludicrousness of our society—watching people get beaten up and humiliated on game shows (*I Got the Sh*t Kicked Out of Me*), exalted jobs that broker indentured labor, power callers, and of course . . . Equisapiens. In one memorable scene, the newly minted power caller and picket line scab, Cassius Green, is pegged in the head with a soda can by a striking coworker. The resulting attention makes the coworker rich through multiple endorsements.

1.5 ounces Jack Daniel's Tennessee Whiskey

0.33 ounce Ancho Reyes Verde Chile Poblano Liqueur

Heavy barspoon walnut liqueur (Nux Alpina Walnut Liqueur preferred)

1 barspoon fresh lime juice

2 dashes Bittermens Xocolatl Mole Bitters

Fentimans Curiosity Cola to top

Build all the ingredients in a collins glass, add ice to top, and serve immediately.

In 1991, director Boots Riley was working for the United Parcel Service when he cofounded the political hip-hop group The Coup with fellow UPS worker E-roc (hence the inclusion in our Music Driven chapter). Rounding out the group were rappers Spice 1 and Mopreme Shakur (then known as Mocedes), and the group's DJ, Pam the Funkstress, who joined in 1992.

PAINKILLER | *THE HARDER THEY COME (1972)*

RUM, MORE RUM, SMOKED COCONUT SYRUP, PINEAPPLE, ORANGE, LIME, JERK BITTERS

YIELD: 1 SERVING
GLASSWARE: LARGE GOBLET GLASS
FOR SERVING: BENDY STRAW

The soundtrack throughout this movie really played an "instrumental" role in this cocktail. With the addition of jerk bitters and a smoked coconut syrup, this Painkiller riff will give you a taste of the tropics while you bob along to reggae.

1.5 ounces Smoked Coconut Syrup (recipe follows)

1 ounce Goslings Black Seal Rum

0.75 ounce pineapple juice

0.33 ounce fresh orange juice

2 barspoons fresh lime juice

0.25 ounce Hamilton 151 Rum

2 dashes House-Made Jerk Bitters (recipe follows)

Skewer of fresh pineapple, orange and a brandied cherry for garnish

1. Combine all the ingredients in a mixing tin, shake vigorously for a few seconds, and dump the entire contents into a large ice-filled goblet.

2. Garnish with the skewered fruit and a bendy straw.

SMOKED COCONUT SYRUP   YIELD: 15 TO 20 SERVINGS

16 ounces Pacific Barista Series Coconut Milk

One 15.5-ounce can Coco López cream of coconut

1 cup + 3 tablespoons sugar

3 dashes Angostura Bitters

1 barspoon liquid smoke

1. Combine all the ingredients, except the liquid smoke, in a pot and bring to a boil.

2. Once boiling, lower the heat to a simmer and cook for 10 minutes.

3. Remove from the heat, add the liquid smoke, and once cooled, refrigerate.

HOUSE-MADE JERK BITTERS   YIELD: 3 OUNCES

3 ounces Hamilton 151 Rum

2 barspoons commercial jerk paste (Walkerswood preferred)

1. Combine the rum and jerk paste in a glass container and allow to infuse to taste for 2 to 4 hours.

2. Fine strain the mixture into a clean jar, and store in a cool, dark place.

YOU CAN GET IT IF YOU REALLY WANT | *THE HARDER THEY COME (1972)*

JAMAICAN BEEF PATTY, PEAS, SCOTCH BONNET PEPPER HABANERO HOT SAUCE

YIELD: 12 PATTIES
ALLERGIES: DAIRY, GLUTEN
TOOLS: LARGE PASTRY CUTTER, FOOD PROCESSOR

This movie helped popularize reggae music and was the first mass-released Jamaican film. The beef patty is a Jamaican staple in the States and one of our favorite fast foods found in Brooklyn. The borough is also home to the largest Caribbean parade in the United States, the West Indian American Day Carnival, held every year on Labor Day Weekend.

FOR THE DOUGH
3 cups all-purpose flour, plus more for dusting
½ pound (2 sticks) cold unsalted butter, cut into cubes
1 tablespoon ground turmeric
2 teaspoons kosher salt
1 teaspoon vodka
¾ cup ice-cold water
1 large egg

FOR THE FILLING
2 tablespoons vegetable oil
1 pound ground beef, 20% fat at minimum
½ Spanish onion, minced
4 garlic cloves, minced
1 Scotch bonnet pepper, seeded and minced
1 tablespoon ground allspice
2 teaspoons freshly ground black pepper
2 teaspoons smoked paprika

2 cups low-sodium beef stock
½ cup ketchup
1 cup frozen peas
Salt and freshly ground black pepper
3 scallions, white and green parts, finely sliced
0.5 ounce fresh thyme leaves

FOR THE PATTIES
Flour for dusting
1 large egg, fork-whipped
Habanero hot sauce for serving

This is widely regarded as the film that opened the doors of the world to reggae, in the same way that the Brazilian film *Black Orpheus* did to introduce bossa nova to the world 10 years earlier.

The beef patty, along with jerk chicken, is one of the main staples of Jamaican food that has migrated from the island. The dough gets its distinct yellow coloring from turmeric.

TO MAKE THE DOUGH

1. In a food processor or by hand, combine the flour, cold butter, turmeric, and salt until it looks like wet sand.

2. Combine the vodka, water, and egg. Slowly add this to the flour mixture until all the liquid is absorbed.

3. Form the dough into a large ball, wrap in plastic, and place in the refrigerator to chill.

TO MAKE THE FILLING

1. While the dough is chilling, heat the vegetable oil in a large cast-iron skillet or Dutch oven, add the ground beef, and let it brown.

2. Once beef is browned, set the meat aside, keeping the fat in the skillet. Add the onions, garlic, and Scotch bonnet to the skillet and sweat until translucent. Then add the allspice, pepper, and paprika and let them toast briefly.

3. Add the beef back to the skillet along with the stock, ketchup, and peas. Bring to a simmer and cook until the broth has thickened and glazes the beef. Season with salt and pepper as needed.

4. Remove the skillet from the heat and add in the scallions and thyme. Place the beef in a bowl to cool completely.

TO MAKE THE PATTIES

1. Preheat the oven to 375°F. Line a baking sheet with parchment paper.

2. When the dough is chilled, remove from the refrigerator and split the dough in half. Rewrap one of the halves and set aside.

3. Dust a large working surface with flour and roll the first half of the dough until ⅛ inch thick. Using a large pastry cutter, cut the dough into rounds.

4. Repeat with the remaining dough.

5. Once the beef mixture has cooled completely, place 2 tablespoons of filling onto one side of the rounds. Fold over and seal with the fork-whipped egg and the back of a fork. Brush the outside of patties with the remaining egg.

6. Place the patties in the oven and bake for 20 to 25 minutes, until golden brown. Let rest for 5 minutes before serving.

7. Serve with habanero hot sauce for how Ivan would have had them.

DTW X CPT PIZZA

SEARCHING FOR SUGAR MAN (2012)

DETROIT-STYLE PIZZA, BOEREWORS SAUSAGE, PERI-PERI SAUCE

YIELD: 1 PIZZA
ALLERGIES: DAIRY, GLUTEN
TOOL: DETROIT-STYLE PIZZA PAN OR A 9-BY-12-INCH NONSTICK METAL BAKING PAN

We've brought a little of South Africa to Detroit with this take on a much-loved regional pizza. As quirky and unexpected as the film, this pizza is a wild ride to enjoy.

Note: If you can't find the bird's eye chiles, you can substitute habanero or other similar chiles to your desired spice level.

FOR THE SAUCE

1 large red onion
6 to 7 garlic cloves, peeled
2 plum tomatoes
2 red bell peppers
6 to 10 bird's eye chiles (see note)
Zest and juice of 2 lemons
¼ cup olive oil
¼ cup red wine vinegar
2 tablespoons granulated sugar
1 tablespoon salt

1 tablespoon freshly ground black pepper
1 tablespoon dried oregano
2 bay leaves

FOR THE SAUSAGE

1 pound ground beef
8 ounces ground pork
1 tablespoon ground coriander
½ teaspoon ground allspice
½ teaspoon freshly ground black pepper
¼ teaspoon ground nutmeg

¼ teaspoon star anise
1 tablespoon dark brown sugar
2 tablespoons malt vinegar
2 teaspoons kosher salt

FOR ASSEMBLY

¼ cup olive oil
1 recipe pizza dough (page 27)
2 to 3 cups freshly grated mozzarella

TO MAKE THE SAUCE

1. Peel and roughly chop the onion and garlic.

2. Cut a shallow X into the nonstem end of the tomatoes and blanch in boiling water for 1 minute. Peel and chop the tomatoes.

3. Char the bell peppers in a broiler or over a gas burner. Transfer to a bowl and cover with plastic wrap. Once cooled, remove and discard the seeds and stems, and roughly chop.

4. Remove the stems from the chiles.

5. Combine all the sauce ingredients in a saucepan and simmer for 20 to 30 minutes. Remove the bay leaves and blend the sauce until smooth.

TO MAKE THE SAUSAGE

Combine all the sausage ingredients in a large, nonreactive bowl and mix well. Cook a small piece in a sauté pan and taste. Adjust the seasoning as needed.

CONTINUED ▶

TO ASSEMBLE THE PIZZA

1. Preheat the oven to 500°F. Pour the olive oil into a Detroit-style pizza pan or a 9-by-12-inch nonstick metal baking pan.

2. Using your fingers, press the dough into the pan until it forms an even layer on the bottom.

3. Spread a thin layer of the sauce over the dough and top with the mozzarella.

4. Drop small bits of the sausage mixture in evenly spaced chunks on top of the cheese.

5. Bake for 14 to 16 minutes, until the edges are black and crispy.

6. Allow to cool and cut into eight squares. Serve with the extra sauce on the side for dipping.

Original pressings of Rodriguez's records regularly sell for over $1,000 when they turn up.

CRIME IN THE CITY | *STYLE WARS (1983)*

RUM, SOUR ORANGE–OREGANO SYRUP, LIME, BEER

YIELD: 1 SERVING
GLASSWARE: BEER GLASS

A drink you might have in the back of a bodega, poured into small plastic cups, with a shot of Brugal rum poured in to make it stronger.

Pro Tip: Listen to the album *Mos Def & Talib Kweli Are Black Star* while fixing yourself the drink and listen for the *Style Wars* reference in the song "Respiration."

1 ounce Brugal 1888 Rum

1.5 ounces Sour Orange–
Oregano Syrup
(recipe follows)

0.25 ounce fresh lime juice

4 ounces extra cold
El Presidente beer

Build all the ingredients into your beer glass, adding a few ice cubes to fill to the top.

SOUR ORANGE–OREGANO SYRUP   YIELD: 2 CUPS

2 sour oranges (if unavailable, substitute 3 tangerines, 4 ounces of fresh orange juice, and 2 ounces of fresh lime juice)

1 cup + 3 tablespoons sugar

8 ounces water

1½ tablespoons fresh oregano

1. Remove the flesh from the sour orange (saving the peels) and blend in a blender until smooth. Fine strain the juice and set aside.

2. Combine the sugar, water, oregano, and the peel of one sour orange in a nonreactive pot and boil for 5 minutes. Remove from the heat and fine strain the syrup.

3. Combine 1 cup of the freshly pressed juice and 1 cup of the syrup in a glass jar and refrigerate.

CONTINUED ▶

Pair with an additional 40 ounces of ice-cold El Presidente beer–poured into a beer glass or straight from the bottle!

The intense competition between graffiti writers, and the risks involved with getting their work on the walls and trains of New York City, was documented for the first time in *Style Wars*, which initially aired on PBS Television, bringing this world to the attention of the uninitiated for the first time. It features many of the most prolific and talented writers of the time including SKEME, pictured below.

TOP 5 RECORDS | *HIGH FIDELITY (2000)*

RYE WHISKEY, GRAPEFRUIT, ORGEAT, LEMON, SUZE, SODA WATER

YIELD: 1 SERVING
ALLERGY: TREE NUTS (ALMOND)
GLASSWARE: HIGHBALL

A tasty cocktail you might whip up for yourself while reorganizing your album collection. Not by chronological or alphabetical order, but in an autobiographical sense . . .

1.5 ounces 100-proof rye whiskey

0.5 ounce grapefruit liqueur (Giffard Crème de Pamplemousse Rose preferred)

0.33 ounce orgeat syrup (Small Hand Foods Orgeat preferred)

0.5 ounce fresh lemon juice

1 barspoon Suze Gentian Liqueur

Splash of soda water

1. Combine all the ingredients, except the soda water, in a mixing tin, add ice, and shake vigorously.
2. Fill a highball glass with ice and add a small amount of fresh soda water to incorporate.
3. Fine strain the cocktail into the glass.

CHAMPIONSHIP VINYL |

HIGH FIDELITY (2000)

HOT DOG, TOMATO, PEPPADEW PEPPERS, KOSHER PICKLE, CELERY SALT, POPPY SEED BUN

YIELD: 4 SERVINGS
ALLERGIES: GLUTEN (POSSIBLY DAIRY OR SOY, DEPENDING ON BUN BRAND; READ LABEL)

Can hot dogs be healthy? This version of a Chicago-style hot dog is as close as you can get! Great for a summer day or binge eating during a breakup.

4 all-beef hot dogs

1 Roma tomato

One 400-gram jar red peppadew peppers

4 poppy seed hot dog buns

Ketchup

Yellow mustard

1 teaspoon celery salt

4 kosher dill pickle spears

1. Pour 2 quarts of water into a 3-quart saucepot, bring to a boil, and add the hot dogs, reducing the heat to a simmer.
2. Slice the Roma tomato into half-moons.
3. Remove half of the peppers from the jar and roughly chop.
4. Lightly toast the hot dog buns.
5. When the hot dogs are hot, start to assemble: Open the bun, alternate ketchup and mustard, place the hot dog on top, then season with the celery salt. Line one side of the dog with one-quarter of the peppadew peppers and slices of the Roma tomato, place the pickle on the other side, and serve!

INTRAVENUS DE MILO | *SPINAL TAP (1984)*

PIMM'S, CUCUMBER, PRESERVED LEMON, RHUBARB/GINGER SYRUP, MINT, SODA WATER

YIELD: 1 SERVING
GLASSWARE: COLLINS GLASS

This drink goes to 11. It has armadillos in its trousers.

2 slices cucumber
2 ounces Pimm's No. 1
**0.25 ounce preserved
   lemon brine**
**1 ounce Rhubarb/Ginger
   Syrup (recipe follows)**
6 fresh mint leaves
Soda water to top
Crown of mint for garnish
**1 foil-covered gherkin
   for garnish**

1. Muddle the cucumber in a cocktail shaker tin, then add all the other ingredients, except the soda and garnishes, and shake well.

2. Strain into an ice-filled collins glass and top with soda water.

3. Garnish with the crown of mint and foil-covered gherkin.

RHUBARB/GINGER SYRUP YIELD: 1 CUP

1½ cups sugar
1 cup chopped rhubarb
**One 1-inch knob fresh
   ginger, chopped**
1 cup water

1. Combine all the ingredients in a pot, bring to a light boil, lower the heat, and simmer for 15 minutes.

2. Allow to cool completely, then strain.

In an unbelievable case of life imitating art, Black Sabbath had a Stonehenge set constructed for their 1983 Born Again tour, which as a result of getting meters and feet confused in the measurements, was too big to fit on the stage.

LET'S GO CRAZY | *PURPLE RAIN (1984)*

FRIED MINNESOTAN CHEESE CURD, PURPLE BEET KETCHUP, PINK CITRIC SALT, EDIBLE GOLD LEAF

YIELD: 4 SERVINGS
ALLERGIES: DAIRY, EGG, GLUTEN
TOOLS: CHEESECLOTH; LARGE, HEAVY-BOTTOMED POT; HIGH-POWERED BLENDER

With the movie taking place in Prince's birthplace and it being semi-autobiographical, we took a classic Minnesotan dish and made it princely. Beets make the ketchup purple, and the sea salt and gold leaf make it sparkle.

FOR THE PURPLE BEET KETCHUP

- 4½ pounds purple beets
- 1½ tablespoons + 2 teaspoons salt
- 2 tablespoons chopped fresh cilantro
- 2 lemons
- 2 medium purple onions
- 2 medium apples
- 3 large garlic cloves
- 3 tablespoons sunflower oil
- ⅔ cup sugar
- 2 tablespoons white vinegar
- 2 star anise
- 1 quart water, plus more to cover beets in pan
- 2 tablespoons minced fresh ginger

FOR THE CHEESE CURDS

- 1 pound cheese curds, such as Ellsworth
- 1⅔ cups all-purpose flour
- 2 large eggs
- 1⅓ cups fine bread crumbs
- ⅓ teaspoon salt
- Oil for frying

FOR THE FINISHING SALT

- 1 tablespoon pink Himalayan salt
- ⅛ teaspoon citric acid
- ¼ teaspoon edible gold leaf

TO MAKE THE PURPLE BEET KETCHUP

1. Preheat the oven to 350°F.

2. Rinse the beets and place in a single layer on the bottom of a large baking pan along with 1½ tablespoons of the salt and the cilantro. Slice the lemons in half and add to the pan. Cover the beets with cold water, cover the pan with aluminum foil, and roast in the oven until fork-tender. Remove from the oven, let cool slightly, then peel and slice the beets.

3. Peel and slice the purple onions, apples, and garlic. Heat the oil in a large, nonreactive saucepot and cook the onions, apples, and garlic over low heat until soft. Add the sugar and cook for 2 to 3 minutes more, until the sugar just begins to caramelize. Deglaze with the vinegar and cook for an additional 3 to 5 minutes, until the liquid has reduced and become syrupy.

4. Tie the star anise in a piece of cheesecloth and add to the sauce. Add the sliced beets, 1 quart of water, and the remaining 2 teaspoons of salt. Simmer for 10 minutes. Remove from the heat and remove star anise cheesecloth. Add the ginger and blend well in a high-powered blender in batches until smooth.

CONTINUED ▶

TO MAKE THE CHEESE CURDS

1. Completely coat the cheese curd with three-quarters of the flour.

2. Whisk the eggs in a large bowl and soak the floured curd in the eggs until fully coated.

3. Mix the remaining flour with the bread crumbs and toss egg-coated curds with the mixture until completely covered.

4. Heat 4 inches of the oil to 350°F in a large, heavy-bottomed pot.

5. Fry until golden brown.

TO MAKE THE FINISHING SALT

Blend the salt ingredients and sprinkle onto the cheese curds.

This film based on Prince's own life was a huge success for every division of his label, Warner Brothers, with a hit film, soundtrack, music video, and eventual VHS release.

GASLIGHT | *INSIDE LLEWYN DAVIS (2013)*

BRIOCHE, CARAMELIZED ONIONS, CHEDDAR

YIELD: 4 SERVINGS
TOOLS: WOODEN SPOON, PASTRY BRUSH

Named after the café where the main character plays in beginning of movie, this is a version of the Welsh rarebit—a dish Roland Turner talks about after learning of Llewyn's Welsh background.

FOR THE CARAMELIZED ONIONS

2 large yellow onions, peeled (about 1 pound)
2 tablespoons unsalted butter
Pinch of kosher salt
½ cup low-sodium chicken stock or water for pan (optional)

FOR THE RAREBIT

1 brioche loaf, sliced 2 inches thick
2 tablespoons unsalted butter, melted
8 ounces white Cheddar
3 tablespoons thinly sliced fresh chives

TO MAKE THE CARAMELIZED ONIONS

1. Slice the onions in half, place one onion half on your cutting board so its root end is facing you, then thinly slice the onion lengthwise, starting at one side and working all the way to the other (so your knife runs halfway through the root, not starting or ending at the root end). You're going for slices that are ¼ to ⅛ inch thick.

2. Repeat the same slicing procedure for remaining onion halves. It's a lot of onion! But it will cook down quite a bit, so it's best to start with a large quantity.

3. Heat the butter in a large saucepan over medium heat until melted and sizzling. (Alternatively, you can use a skillet to cook the onion, but a pan with high sides will keep the onions from flipping out onto your stove. Using a pan that also has a wide base gives water room to evaporate, allowing the onion to caramelize rather than steam.)

4. Instead of dumping in all of the onion at once, which would fill the pot and make it hard to stir (which would then cause the ones on the bottom to cook faster), start by adding just a couple of large handfuls to the pot. Cook, stirring, until the onions are soft and starting to turn translucent, 1 to 2 minutes. Stir in a few more handfuls of onion and repeat the cooking and stirring process until you've added all of the onion. Season with a pinch of salt.

5. Lower the heat to medium-low and continue to cook the onion, stirring every few minutes to prevent sticking and coloring too much in any one place, until blond colored, 15 to 20 minutes. Keep cooking, stirring on the regular, until the onion is unmistakably golden brown, another 15 to 20 minutes. Because most of the water has cooked off at this point, there might be some bare spots where the pot could start to burn. If this happens, stir in a splash of stock or water. The liquid will dissolve the cooked-on bits, which the onion will reabsorb.

CONTINUED ▶

Welsh rarebit is a Welsh dish consisting of a hot cheese-based sauce served over slices of toasted bread. The original 18th-century name of the dish was the jocular "Welsh rabbit," which was later reinterpreted as "rarebit," as the dish contains no rabbit.

TO MAKE THE RAREBIT

1. Preheat the broiler. Place a sauté pan over medium-high heat on the stovetop.

2. Brush each side of the brioche bread with the melted butter. Place on the pan and let brown, then flip and brown the second side.

3. Once toasted, place a spoonful of caramelized onions on the bread.

4. Grate the white Cheddar on top to cover.

5. Place the finished slices of bread on a baking sheet and place in the oven, 8 to 10 inches from the broiler.

6. Let cook until the cheese is melted and starting to brown.

7. Remove and sprinkle with the chives.

Joel Coen was quoted saying, "The film doesn't really have a plot. That concerned us at one point; that's why we threw the cat in."

ZOOT SUIT | *QUADROPHENIA (1979)*

GIN, CAMPARI, COFFEE-INFUSED VERMOUTH

YIELD: 1 SERVING
GLASSWARE: ROCKS GLASS

This is a variation on a Negroni. It is a reference to the mod culture's appropriation of Italian fashion and mopeds. The mod scene in London was centered on coffee bars, and the coffee is also a reference to their use of uppers. Best paired with a white jacket with 5-inch side vents.

1 ounce Beefeater London Dry Gin
1 ounce Campari
1 ounce Coffee-Infused Vermouth (recipe follows)
Orange peel for garnish

1. Combine all the ingredients, except the orange peel, in an ice-filled mixing glass.
2. Stir and strain over ice into a rocks glass.
3. Garnish with the orange peel.

COFFEE-INFUSED VERMOUTH

1 cup whole dark roast coffee beans
One 750-milliliter bottle sweet vermouth

Combine the coffee beans and sweet vermouth in a nonreactive container, allow to infuse for 24 hours, and then strain.

John Lydon (a.k.a Johnny Rotten from the Sex Pistols) was originally approached for the role of Jimmy and even did a screen test. However, the distributors refused to insure him for the part and he was replaced with Phil Daniels.

WHEEL OF FISH | *UHF* (1989)

RED SNAPPER, PISTACHIO PESTO, MORNAY SAUCE

YIELD: 4 SERVINGS
ALLERGIES: DAIRY, EGG, FISH, GLUTEN, TREE NUTS (PISTACHIO)
TOOLS: FOOD PROCESSOR, 4 TOOTHPICKS

Inspired by one of the most ridiculous scenes in movie history, the wheel of fish game show. To contrast with the low budget and low comedy of the film, we made an elevated, literal, wheel of fish.

FOR THE PINWHEEL FILLING

Oil for casserole dish

2 garlic cloves, minced

1 bunch parsley

⅛ cup minced fresh chives

12 ounces roasted pistachios

1 cup panko bread crumbs

1 large egg

Zest and juice of 1 lemon

¼ teaspoon freshly
  ground black pepper

Four 4-ounce skinned
  red snapper fillets

Salt

FOR THE MORNAY SAUCE

6 tablespoons (¾ stick)
  unsalted butter

⅔ cup all-purpose flour

3 cups milk, at room
  temperature

3 cloves

¼ onion

1 bay leaf

Freshly grated nutmeg

3.5 ounces Gruyère, shredded

Salt

> The script originally called for swordfish, but it wasn't available at the fish market that morning. They went with red snapper instead.

TO MAKE THE PINWHEEL FILLING

1. Preheat the oven to 325°F.

2. Prepare a casserole dish with a small amount of oil on the bottom.

3. Combine the garlic, parsley, chives, pistachios, panko, egg, lemon zest (reserving the juice), and pepper in a food processor. Pulse until a consistent texture.

4. Take each filet and butterfly cut through the middle to make a long, even surface. Season lightly with salt

5. Evenly spread the pistachio mixture over each fillet, leaving 1 inch of fish bare at one end.

6. Firmly roll up the fish into a spiral and secure with a toothpick.

7. Place the fish rolls in the prepared casserole dish and bake for 15 to 20 minutes, until the fish is flaky.

8. Remove the fish rolls from the oven and sprinkle with the reserved lemon juice.

9. Serve with a mystery box containing absolutely nothing.

TO MAKE THE MORNAY SAUCE

1. Melt the butter in a pot over low heat.

2. Whisk in the flour and cook until barely bubbling.

3. Slowly whisk in the milk.

4. Push the cloves into the onion and add to the pot along with the bay leaf.

5. Add a small amount of freshly grated nutmeg to the pot.

6. Allow to simmer until reduced by a third, stirring occasionally.

7. Whisk in the Gruyère until melted.

8. Add salt to taste and drizzle on top of the fish.

CONTINUED ▷

For the shot of the Spatula City billboard, the production bought a billboard on a remote stretch of highway. For months afterward, drivers taking the exit would ask nearby businesses about Spatula City. The ad was finally removed after the businesses complained.

DOUBLE-THYME SLING | *WHIPLASH (2014)*

GIN, SWEET VERMOUTH, THYME SYRUP, BITTERS, SODA WATER

YIELD: 1 SERVING
GLASSWARE: HIGHBALL GLASS

Inspired by the modern Sling recipe, thyme is used both as a garnish and in the simple syrup to make it a double thyme, a play on the double-time swing from the film.

1.5 ounces gin
1 ounce sweet vermouth
0.75 ounce fresh lemon juice
0.75 ounce Thyme Syrup
  (recipe follows)
2 dashes Angostura Bitters
2 ounces soda water
1 sprig thyme for garnish

1. Combine all the ingredients, except the soda and garnish, in an ice-filled cocktail shaker tin.
2. Shake and strain over ice into a highball glass.
3. Add the soda water and garnish with the sprig of thyme.

THYME SYRUP YIELD: 1 CUP

1 cup water
1 cup + 2 tablespoons sugar
10 sprigs thyme

1. Combine the water and sugar in a pan.
2. Bring just to a boil, lower the heat to low, add the thyme sprigs. simmer for 20 minutes, then strain.

CONTINUED ▶

WHIPLASH FOOD BONUS

THE USUAL: BUTTERED POPCORN, RAISINETS

You don't have to settle for microwave popcorn! Making it at home is easier than it looks and you end up with a better product! All you need are popcorn kernels, a good pot with a lid, oil, and salt. Adding a box of Raisinets means you can join Jim and Andrew Nieman in their usual movie ritual.

ART SEEN:

VISUAL ART TAKES CENTER FRAME

There are many different ways art finds itself in the movies. Of course, film is an art form in itself, but something special happens when visual art is at the center of the story. Whether it's inspired by the extraordinary life of a painter as in *Basquiat* or a fictional caper about a stolen painting as in Wes Anderson's *The Grand Budapest Hotel*, or presenting experimental artist videos from the 1960s outside the gallery, Art Seen celebrates the marriage of art and film.

THE RHYTHM AND POETRY OF LIFE | *BEFORE NIGHT FALLS (2000)*

CUBAN AGUARDIENTE, HONEY, KEY LIME

YIELD: 1 SERVING
GLASSWARE: ROCKS GLASS

A film based on an autobiography written by Reinaldo Arenas, a Cuban poet, novelist, and playwright known as an early sympathizer and later critic of Fidel Castro and the Cuban Revolution, and a rebel of the Cuban government. This is a Canchanchara cocktail, considered Cuba's original cocktail.

0.5 ounce raw honey

1.5 ounces water

0.5 ounce fresh Key lime juice

2 ounces Cuban aguardiente (white rum, such as Havana Club 3 Años, can be substituted)

Fresh sugarcane for garnish (optional)

1. Mix the honey with the water and lime juice and spread the mixture on the bottom and sides of a rocks glass.
2. Add cracked ice and then top with the aguardiente.
3. Stir vigorously and garnish with fresh sugarcane, if using.

The Canchanchara cocktail was named after the leather-covered flask used by the Cuban guerrillas fighting in the Ten Years' War and the War of Independence against the Spanish.

After a career spanning more than 25 years in television and film, this was Javier Bardem's first English-speaking role.

BLOW-UP | *BLOW-UP* (1966)

VANILLA-INFUSED APEROL, PROSECCO, LAVENDER BITTERS, LEMON, SODA WATER

YIELD: 1 SERVING
GLASSWARE: HIGHBALL GLASS

Another classic Italian cocktail variation inspired by the English mod appropriation of Italian culture. This Aperol spritz has vanilla and lavender, two floral ingredients that are a nod to the Maryon Park setting of the photographs in the film.

1.5 ounces Vanilla-Infused Aperol (recipe follows)
1.5 ounces Prosecco
1.5 ounces soda water
0.25 ounce fresh lemon juice
2 dashes lavender bitters
Orange peel for garnish

1. Combine all the ingredients , except the garnish, in an ice-filled mixing glass.
2. Stir and strain over ice into a highball glass.
3. Garnish with the orange peel.

VANILLA-INFUSED APEROL

1 vanilla bean
One 750-milliliter bottle Aperol

1. Split the vanilla bean lengthwise with a knife and add to the bottle of Aperol.
2. Let sit for 24 hours and strain.

The film contains a rare performance of the Yardbirds performing "Train Kept A-Rollin'" during the period when Jimmy Page (who would go on to form Led Zeppelin) and Jeff Beck were both in the band. Beck would leave a few months later.

RED RIGHT HAND

20,000 DAYS ON EARTH (2014)

SCOTCH, BÄRENJÄGER, LEMON, EARL GREY SYRUP, SHIRAZ

YIELD: 1 SERVING
GLASSWARE: ROCKS GLASS

This film finds Nick Cave contemplating the meaning of the 20,000 days he has spent on Earth. This cocktail pulls references and ingredients from the places he spent time, including Victoria, Berlin, and Brighton.

2 ounces single malt Scotch
0.25 ounce Bärenjäger
0.75 ounce fresh lemon juice
0.5 ounce Earl Grey Tea Syrup (recipe follows)
1 ounce Shiraz to top

1. Combine all the ingredients in an ice-filled cocktail mixing tin.
2. Shake and strain into an ice-filled rocks glass.
3. Gently pour the Shiraz on top of the cocktail.

EARL GREY TEA SYRUP YIELD: 1 CUP

1 cup sugar
1 cup water
2 ounces Earl Grey tea leaves

1. Combine all the ingredients in a nonreactive pot and bring to a boil.
2. Turn off the heat, allow to steep for 20 minutes, then strain.

In addition to penning the screenplay for *20,000 Days on Earth*, Nick Cave has written the screenplay for *The Proposition* (2005) and *Lawless* (2012). He was asked by Russell Crowe to write a proposed sequel to *Gladiator* (2000), which was never produced.

A BUCKET OF BLOOD

A BUCKET OF BLOOD (1959)

VODKA, TOMATO, LEMON, WORCESTERSHIRE, PEPPER, CELERY SALT, SRIRACHA, HORSERADISH, PICKLE

YIELD: 1 SERVING
ALLERGY: FISH (OR CHOOSE VEGAN WORCESTERSHIRE)
GLASSWARE: 16-OUNCE FOOD-SAFE BUCKET (STAINLESS STEEL)

A literal bucket of Bloody Mary. Tastes better than real blood.

2 ounces vodka

6 ounces Bloody Mary Mix (recipe follows)

1 garlic clove

2 ounces fresh lemon juice

46 ounces tomato juice

3.75 ounces Worcestershire sauce

2 teaspoons freshly ground black pepper

1 teaspoon celery salt

1 teaspoon kosher salt

1 tablespoon sriracha

1 tablespoon prepared horseradish

2 ounces pickle juice

1 teaspoon liquid smoke (optional)

2 ounces vodka

1. In a blender, blend together the garlic and lemon juice until smooth. Then add all the other ingredients, except the vodka, and blend again.

2. Add 6 ounces of the blended mixture to an ice-filled 16-ounce bucket. Add the vodka and mix well.

The film was shot in five days on a budget of only $50,000. At the time of its original release, there was a promotion in the newspaper movie section advertisements that made the offer, "If You Bring in a Bucket of Blood to Your Local Theater's Management (or Ticket Booth), You Will Be Given One Free Admission."

Around 1920, at Harry's New York Bar in Paris, bartender Ferdinand "Pete" Petiot started experimenting with new cocktails made with vodka, thanks to an influx of Russian immigrants who had left their country during the revolution. After adding a few extra flavors, such as Worcestershire sauce, black pepper, and lemon, the "first" Bloody Mary was born. According to Esquire, Ernest Hemingway was a well-known patron at Harry's and particularly loved the Bloody Mary.

Petiot then traveled to New York City to work at the King Cole Bar at the St. Regis Hotel, where a drink called the Red Snapper gained popularity. Over the years, the Bloody Mary garnish game has evolved to ridiculous proportions.

PALETTE KNIFE AND A BUTTERCREAM FLOURISH | *THE GRAND BUDAPEST HOTEL (2014)*

COURTESAN AU CHOCOLAT

YIELD: 6 SERVINGS
ALLERGIES: DAIRY, EGG, GLUTEN

The courtesan au chocolat is the specialty of Mendl's, the pastry shop in the movie. It is asked for by name, and it is the treat that is used to hide the tools for the prison escape. This is nearly the same recipe as on the DVD commentary, but white chocolate is substituted for the glaze to aid in its durability for service in a dark movie theater.

FOR THE CHOUX PASTRY

1 cup water

8 tablespoons (1 stick) unsalted butter

⅛ teaspoon granulated sugar

Pinch of salt

1 cup all-purpose flour, sifted

4 large eggs, beaten

FOR THE CHOCOLATE PASTRY CREAM

1½ cups milk

90 ounces (5 pounds 10 ounces) semisweet chocolate

3 large egg yolks

¼ cup granulated sugar

2 tablespoons unsweetened cocoa powder

1 tablespoon all-purpose flour

1 teaspoon cornstarch

FOR THE WHITE CHOCOLATE TOPPING

1 pound white chocolate

¼ cup heavy cream

Drops of red, green, and blue *oil-based* food coloring

FOR THE BUTTERCREAM

1 cup confectioners' sugar

5 tablespoons unsalted butter, at room temperature

⅓ teaspoon vanilla extract

1 teaspoon heavy cream

Blue food coloring

TO MAKE THE CHOUX PASTRY

1. Preheat the oven to 350°F. Line a baking sheet with parchment paper.

2. Combine the water, butter, granulated sugar, and salt in a large saucepan and bring to a boil.

3. Mix in the sifted flour until a paste forms.

4. Remove from the heat and allow to cool enough that it will not cook the eggs—about 120°F.

5. Mix in the eggs.

6. Transfer the batter to a pastry bag fitted with a ½-inch straight tip.

7. Pipe out three differently sized balls (3 inches, 2 inches, and 1 inch).

CONTINUED ▶

8. Bake for 25 to 35 minutes, until golden brown.

9. While still hot, poke holes in the bottom of the choux to allow the steam to vent.

TO MAKE THE CHOCOLATE PASTRY CREAM

1. Place the milk and chocolate in a large pot and heat slowly over low heat, stirring, until the chocolate has fully melted and combined with the milk.

2. Meanwhile, in a bowl, whisk together the egg yolks, granulated sugar, cocoa powder, flour, and cornstarch into a paste.

3. Temper the egg mixture by slowly adding the chocolate mixture. Once fully combined, transfer to the pot and cook until a custard consistency is reached and the mixture coats the back of a spoon—about 170°F.

4. Pour the mixture into separate heatproof container and cover with plastic wrap, allowing the wrap to gently touch the surface.

5. Let cool completely.

6. Transfer into a pastry bag with ¼-inch tip snipped off and fill all three choux pastries.

TO MAKE THE WHITE CHOCOLATE TOPPING

1. Place the white chocolate in a heatproof bowl. Heat the cream in a small pot until simmering and pour over the chocolate.

2. Stir until the chocolate has melted.

3. Separate into three different bowls and mix in food coloring to achieve your desired colors.

4. Dip the choux balls as follows: large balls, purple; medium, pink; small, green

5. Set aside to cool.

TO MAKE THE BUTTERCREAM

1. Mix all the buttercream ingredients together in a large bowl.

2. Transfer to a pastry bag with ¼-inch tip snipped off.

3. Pipe a small amount onto each ball to use to fasten the balls together: one of each size stacked from large to small.

The chocolate brings out the Wes Anderson color palette as well as helps this delicate dessert survive its journey from our kitchen to the cinema seats.

To let the viewer know which time period was taking place (1985, 1968, and 1932), the film was shot in three different aspect ratios: 1.85:1, 2.35:1, and 1.37:1.

TOWER OF BABEL | *BASQUIAT (1996)*

DARK CHOCOLATE CAKE DOUGHNUTS, VANILLA RUM ROYAL ICING

YIELD: 4 SERVINGS
ALLERGIES: DAIRY, GLUTEN
TOOLS: ROLLING PIN, DOUGHNUT CUTTER OR RING MOLDS, SLOTTED SPOON, WIDE FOOD-GRADE PAINTBRUSH

Made to resemble the tower of car tires with a line painted down it that is envisioned and later created by Basquiat.

FOR THE DOUGHNUTS

3 tablespoons unsalted butter, at room temperature

1¼ cups sugar

4 large egg yolks (save egg whites for icing)

16 ounces sour cream

3½ cups all-purpose flour

1 cup dark cocoa powder

1 tablespoons baking powder

1 teaspoon salt

¼ cup dark chocolate chips

3 quarts canola oil

FOR THE ICING

2½ cups confectioners' sugar

1.5 ounces (about 3 tablespoons) egg whites

1½ teaspoons clear vanilla extract

1½ teaspoons white rum

¼ teaspoon salt

⅛ teaspoon cream of tartar

¼ cup heavy cream

TO MAKE THE DOUGHNUTS

1. Combine the butter and sugar in the bowl of a stand mixer fitted with the paddle attachment and mix on medium speed for 2 minutes.

2. Add the egg yolks, one at a time, until fully combined.

3. Add the sour cream until fully combined.

4. Stir together the flour, cocoa powder, baking powder, and salt in a large separate bowl.

5. Slowly add the flour mixture to the egg mixture and turn off the mixer as soon as combined. Stir in the chocolate chips by hand.

6. Cover the bowl and chill in the refrigerator for 1 hour.

7. When chilled, transfer the dough to a clean counter and roll out to 1-inch thickness.

8. Using either a doughnut cutter or a 3-inch and a 1-inch ring mold, cut into doughnuts and set on a parchment-lined baking sheet.

9. Put back into the refrigerator for 30 minutes.

10. Heat the oil to 350°F in a 6-quart pot.

11. Carefully lower the doughnuts into the oil, working in batches, being sure to drop them away from yourself.

12. Let cook for 1½ minutes per side, flipping with a slotted spoon.

13. When crispy on both sides, remove from the oil with the slotted spoon and transfer to a wire rack to cool.

CONTINUED ▶

TO MAKE THE ICING

1. Bring about 2 inches of water to a boil in a medium pot.

2. In a nonreactive metal bowl that can sit on the pot without its base touching the water, mix together 1 cup of the confectioners' sugar and the egg whites, vanilla, rum, salt, and cream of tartar until smooth.

3. Place on top of the simmering pot and stir with a spatula until it reaches 150°F.

4. Remove from the heat and whisk in the remaining 1½ cups of confectioners' sugar

5. Whisk in the heavy cream until the mixture has a paintlike consistency

TO ASSEMBLE

1. Pour a thin layer of icing on the bottom of a plate.

2. Stack three to five doughnuts on top of each other with a thin layer of icing between them to hold them together.

3. With a wide, food-safe paintbrush, paint a thick layer of icing down one side of the stack

4. Be inspired by your art.

David Bowie wore actual wigs that had belonged to Andy Warhol and went to a record store in full costume during a break in filming, which caused quite a stir.

SOME THINGS ARE MORE IMPORTANT THAN PIT BEEF | *PECKER* (1998)

BALTIMORE-STYLE PIT BEEF, SPANISH ONION, HORSERADISH, YELLOW MUSTARD, KAISER ROLL

YIELD: 4 SERVINGS
ALLERGIES: DAIRY, GLUTEN
TOOLS: GRILL, MANDOLINE (OPTIONAL)

You from the city or the county? Doesn't matter because this thinly sliced pit beef stacked high on a kaiser roll is as Baltimore as it gets. Remember to warsh your hands before enjoying!

FOR THE PIT BEEF

2 pounds tri-tip or
   top round beef
3 tablespoons kosher salt
1 tablespoon smoked paprika
1 teaspoon freshly
   ground black pepper
1 tablespoon dried oregano

FOR THE SANDWICHES

1 Spanish onion
4 kaiser rolls
¼ cup prepared horseradish
¼ cup prepared yellow mustard

> Pit beef is Baltimore's version of barbecue, usually made with top round and kept on an open charcoal pit grill and slowly grilled all day, with the large pieces being slowly whittled down throughout the course of the day.

TO MAKE THE PIT BEEF

1. Rub the beef with all the spices and let marinate in a dish covered with plastic wrap for a minimum of 3 hours and a maximum of 48.

2. Prepare a hot grill, preferably using charcoal.

3. Grill the steak until it reaches a 130°F internal temperature, turning often to ensure a crust of spices on the outside of the steak.

4. Remove from the grill and let the steak rest for 15 to 20 minutes before slicing, as thinly as possible (use a slicer if you have one), against the grain.

TO MAKE THE SANDWICHES

1. While the steak is grilling, slice the onion very thinly on a mandoline. For a more muted onion flavor, soak the sliced onion in an ice water bath for 10 to 15 minutes, then blot dry with a paper towel.

2. Gently toast each kaiser roll on the grill.

3. Build each sandwich by starting on the bottom with 1 tablespoon of the horseradish, 1 tablespoon of yellow mustard, one-quarter of the sliced steak, five or six onion rings, and then the top of the roll.

CONTINUED ▷

John Waters briefly attended New York University's film school but was expelled for smoking marijuana on campus. He returned back home to Baltimore, where he made *Roman Candles* (1966)—his first film to star both Divine and the future cast of *Pink Flamingos* (1972).

AIR OF QUIET DEATH

PHANTOM THREAD (2017)

MUSHROOM-INFUSED GIN, LAPSANG-INFUSED VERMOUTH

YIELD: 1 SERVING
GLASSWARE: COUPE GLASS

A marrying of Woodcock's drinks of choice: a gin martini and lapsang souchong tea. Of course spiked with mushrooms for a savory and complex martini variation.

---

2 ounces Mushroom-Infused Plymouth Gin (recipe follows)

0.75 ounce Lapsang-Infused Vermouth (recipe follows)

Lemon peel for garnish

1. Combine all the ingredients in an ice-filled mixing glass.
2. Stir and strain into a coupe glass.
3. Garnish with the lemon peel.

MUSHROOM-INFUSED PLYMOUTH GIN YIELD: 1 LITER

1 liter Plymouth Gin
2 dried shiitake mushrooms
2 dried wood ear mushrooms
Peel of 1 lemon

1. Combine all the ingredients in a glass or food-safe container, first squeezing the peels before adding them.
2. Allow to sit for 1½ hours, then strain and pour back into the bottle.

LAPSANG-INFUSED VERMOUTH YIELD: 750 MILLILITERS

One 750-milliliter bottle Dolin Blanc Vermouth de Chambéry
2 tablespoons lapsang souchong tea

1. Combine the vermouth and tea in a glass or food-safe container.
2. Allow to sit for 1½ hours and then strain.

CONTINUED ▶

Director Paul Thomas Anderson, a fan of Jordan Peele's television work, was shooting this film in London during the winter. In a miserable, depressed period for the director, he went to see Peele's *Get Out* (2017). Anderson was inspired by the film and said that it had made him feel a connection, although rather ironically, back home to America. Peele later saw *Phantom Thread*, which he really took to. Anderson interviewed Peele about the latter's latest horror film, *Us* (2019), in *Fangoria* magazine.

CELERY HAMBURGER, USHIO STYLE | *CUTIE AND THE BOXER* (2013)

CELERY, SHIITAKE HAMBURGER, MISO GRAVY, KATSUOBUSHI

YIELD: 8 SERVINGS
ALLERGIES: DAIRY, GLUTEN, FISH

This is a dinner that Ushio makes for his family. The ripping of the celery into chunks is similar to his art style. Rather than being chopped evenly and finely, it is purposefully uneven, creating a new experience in every bite. The shiitake, miso gravy, and katsuobushi give a literal "punch" of umami.

6 shiitake mushrooms

1 celery stalk

2½ pounds ground beef

2 large eggs

1 cup panko bread crumbs

1 tablespoon soy sauce

Salt and freshly ground black pepper

2 tablespoons unsalted butter

3 tablespoons + 1 teaspoon all-purpose flour

1 cup beef stock

2 teaspoons miso paste

2 tablespoons oil

Katsuobushi

1. Rip the shiitake and celery by hand into bite-size pieces and put in a bowl with the ground beef.

2. In a separate bowl, mix together the eggs, panko, and soy sauce.

3. Blend the beef and egg mixtures together by hand. Add salt and pepper to taste.

4. Refrigerate.

5. Melt the butter in a small pot over low heat and then whisk in the flour to make a roux.

6. Slowly whisk in the beef stock.

7. Whisk in the miso and cook until it coats the back of a spoon. Remove from the heat and keep warm.

8. Separate the meat mixture into eight equal portions and form into patties.

9. Heat the oil in a skillet until sizzling.

10. Cook the burgers to your desired doneness.

11. Serve with the miso mixture on top and with grated katsuobushi.

CONTINUED ▶

> In 1908, umami was first identified by Japanese scientist Dr. Kikunae Ikeda. He named it *umami*, which means "essence of deliciousness" in Japanese. The taste of umami is attributed to glutamate.

Ushio Shinohara has been married to artist Noriko Shinohara since the early 1970s. Together they have a son who is also an artist, Alexander Kūkai Shinohara. The family is based in the DUMBO neighborhood of Brooklyn.

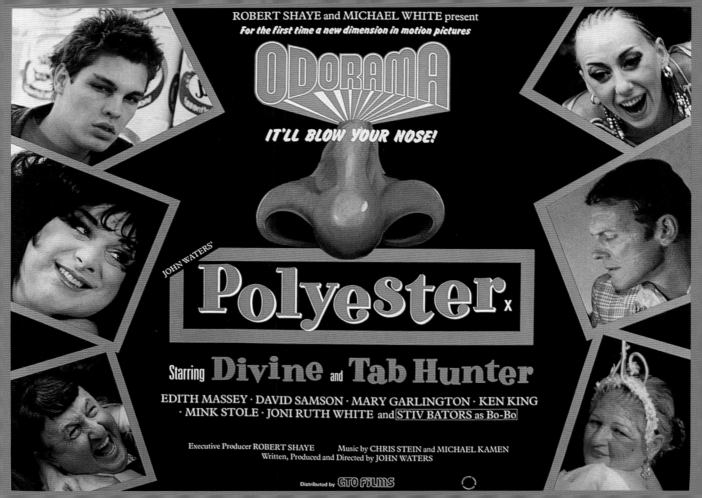

FILM FEAST:

A POTLUCK OF CUISINE INSPIRED SCENE BY SCENE

In a long-standing tradition of upping the ante for the moviegoing experience, it all started with William Castle and *The Tingler* and his "Percepto!" gimmick in the late 1950s. Random theater seats within the auditorium were wired to vibrate or pulse with electricity at critical moments in the film, such as when Vincent Price warns you to "scream—scream for your lives." The effect was electric, and several audience members ran from the theaters in fear.

Pushing things in another direction around the same time, AromaRama and Smell-O-Vision were launched in theaters for two competing movies, *Behind the Great Wall* and *Scent of Mystery* respectively, dubbed "the battle of the smellies" by *Variety*. Scents were pumped into the auditoriums at various scenes to experience the film through your sense of smell. John Waters paid homage in the early 1980s, releasing the film *Polyester* with an "Odorama" version and an accompanying scratch-and-sniff card. Consider this chapter a delicious way to break the fourth wall through Taste-O-Vision!

IF YOU COULD ONLY
HAVE SEEN . . .

BLADE RUNNER

TEARS IN
THE RAIN

AND NOODLES

GIVE ME 4

TAFFEY LEWIS'S 4TH SECTOR, CHINATOWN

I THINK, THEREFORE I AM

ONE ON THE HOUSE

GIVE ME 4 | *BLADE RUNNER (1982)*

SCOTCH, LAPSANG-INFUSED PUNT E MES, UME PLUM, BITTERS

YIELD: 1 SERVING
GLASSWARE: ROCKS GLASS

Inspired by the vision of an Asian-influenced cultural diaspora of future Los Angeles, Deckard's drink of choice, Johnnie Walker, is reimagined in this smoky, Asian-themed Manhattan.

2 ounces Johnnie Walker
   Black Label Scotch Whiskey
0.5 ounce Lapsang-Infused
   Punt e Mes (recipe follows)
0.5 ounce ume plum wine
2 dashes Angostura Bitters
Orange peel for garnish

1. Combine all the ingredients, except the garnish, in an ice-filled mixing glass.
2. Stir and strain into an ice-filled rocks glass.
3. Garnish with an expressed orange peel.

LAPSANG-INFUSED PUNT E MES   **YIELD:** 750 MILLILITERS

One 750-milliliter
   bottle Punt e Mes
2 tablespoons lapsang
   souchong tea

1. Combine the ingredients in a glass or food-safe container.
2. Allow to sit for 1½ hours and then strain.

At least seven different versions of the film exist, with the final cut released on DVD in 2007. This all began after a disastrous preview screening before the summer 1982 release. Although now widely regarded as a classic, the film failed to find an audience, but VHS rentals in the years that followed allowed rewatching and a fan base developed.

AND NOODLES | *BLADE RUNNER* (1982)

SZECHUAN-STYLE IMPOSSIBLE SAUSAGE, DAN DAN NOODLES, VEGAN DEMI

YIELD: 4 SERVINGS
ALLERGIES: GLUTEN, SOY
TOOL: MANDOLINE

Enjoy a big bowl of noodles along with Rick.

FOR THE VEGAN DEMI

4 ounces white mushrooms

¼ Spanish onion

1 garlic clove

1 celery stalk

1 small carrot

1 small canned red beet

1 tablespoon tomato paste

2 tablespoons canola oil

3 cups water

2 tablespoons white miso paste

2 tablespoons soy sauce

FOR THE IMPOSSIBLE SAUSAGE

6 tablespoons canola oil

1 garlic clove, minced

2 tablespoons minced ginger

2 scallions, sliced thinly

1½ pounds Impossible meat

2 tablespoons Chinese five-spice powder

1 teaspoon Szechuan peppercorns, ground after measuring

1 tablespoon kosher salt

FOR SERVING

One 22-ounce package frozen dan dan (thin, egg-free wheat) or lo mein noodles

1 scallion, sliced thinly for garnish

1 tablespoon toasted sesame seeds for garnish

TO MAKE THE VEGAN DEMI

1. Preheat the oven to 375°F. Thinly slice all the vegetables with a mandoline, then toss with the tomato paste and oil. Roast for 30 minutes, or until the vegetables are very browned, bordering on burned.

2. Add the water to the pan along with the miso paste and soy sauce and return to the oven to roast for another 30 to 45 minutes.

3. Carefully remove the pan from the oven and strain the vegetable mixture through a fine-mesh strainer or a colander lined with a coffee filter. Discard the vegetables.

4. Put the strained liquid into a saucepot and bring to a simmer. Reduce slowly until about half of the volume has evaporated and the sauce has thickened slightly. Keep warm until you are ready to serve.

TO MAKE THE SAUSAGE

1. Heat 2 tablespoons of the canola oil in a small sauté pan and sweat the garlic, ginger, and scallions until translucent, then remove from the heat and let cool completely.

2. Combine all of the rest of the ingredients, except the remaining canola oil, in a bowl and mix thoroughly.

3. Heat the remaining 4 tablespoons of canola oil in a cast-iron skillet or large sauté pan and cook the Impossible sausage until well browned. Remove from the heat and set aside along with any remaining liquid left in the pan.

TO SERVE

1. Bring 6 quarts of water to a boil and cook the noodles according to the package instructions.

2. Combine the cooked Impossible sausage, the cooked dan dan noodles, and enough sauce to coat the noodles and sausage in a large mixing bowl.

3. Serve in a large bowl topped with the sliced scallions and toasted sesame seeds.

IF YOU COULD ONLY HAVE SEEN . . . | *BLADE RUNNER* (1982)

IMPOSSIBLE TARTARE, CORNICHONS, CAPERS, BEETS, PARSLEY, DIJON MUSTARD

YIELD: 4 SERVINGS
ALLERGIES: DAIRY, GLUTEN, SOY

This replicant of a traditional beef tartare might be better than the original.

---

1 baguette, sliced on the bias

4 tablespoons (½ stick) unsalted butter, melted

1 pound Impossible meat

1 shallot, minced, or ¼ cup minced red onion

2 garlic cloves, minced

¼ cup cornichons, minced after measuring

2 tablespoons capers, roughly chopped

½ (10-ounce) can whole beets, minced

¼ cup chopped flat-leaf parsley

2 tablespoons Dijon mustard

Juice of 1 lemon

¼ cup extra virgin olive oil

Salt and freshly ground black pepper

> The beets in the recipe are there to give the tartare that iron flavor that you get in a traditional beef tartare.

1. Preheat the oven to 350°F.

2. Brush the sliced baguette with the melted butter and toast in the oven until crispy and golden brown.

3. Very gently mix together all the remaining ingredients in a bowl, seasoning with salt and pepper to taste. Chill and keep very cold until ready to serve.

4. Serve the tartare with the toasted baguette.

A replicant is a fictional bioengineered being in the 1982 film *Blade Runner* and in its 2017 sequel, *Blade Runner 2049*. The Nexus series of replicants are virtually identical to adult humans but have superior strength, speed, agility, resilience, and intelligence to varying degrees, depending on the model. Replicants were a driving force for this entire menu, as we wanted to provide meat-based dishes without meat.

ONE ON THE HOUSE | *BLADE RUNNER* (1982)

RUM, MORE RUM, CHINESE FIVE-SPICE SYRUP, LYCHEE, LIME

YIELD: 1 SERVING
GLASSWARE: COUPE GLASS
GARNISH: PINK COCKTAIL
UMBRELLA

Another nod to its setting, Taffey Lewis's tiki-inspired Chinatown bar.

---

1 ounce Jamaican aged rum

1 ounce white rum

0.5 ounce Chinese Five-Spice
Syrup (recipe follows)

1 ounce lychee syrup
(from canned lychees)

0.75 ounce fresh lime juice

1 canned lychee for garnish

1. Combine all the ingredients, except the garnish, in an ice-filled cocktail shaking tin.

2. Shake and strain into a chilled coupe glass.

3. Garnish with a pink umbrella and a lychee.

CHINESE FIVE-SPICE SYRUP YIELD: 1 CUP

1 cup demerara sugar

1 cup water

1 tablespoon Chinese
five-spice powder

1 tablespoon Szechuan
peppercorns

1. Combine all the ingredients in a small saucepot and bring to a boil.

2. Remove from the heat, allow to cool, and then strain.

Szechuan peppercorn is not only spicy but also, when eaten in enough quantity, will actually act as a natural numbing agent.

TAFFEY LEWIS'S 4TH SECTOR, CHINATOWN | *BLADE RUNNER (1982)*

IMPOSSIBLE MESSA'AA, EGGPLANT, RED PEPPER, CORIANDER, CUMIN, CARDAMOM, MARCONA ALMONDS

YIELD: 4 TO 6 SERVINGS
ALLERGIES: SOY, TREE NUTS (ALMOND)

Warmly spiced and deep in flavor with tons of texture, this is a great dish and is even better the next day.

FOR THE IMPOSSIBLE MESSA'AA

2 tablespoons canola oil

½ Spanish onion

3 garlic cloves, minced

4 green cardamom pods, toasted, broken open, and ground

1 teaspoon ground cinnamon

2 teaspoons cumin seeds, toasted and ground

2 teaspoons coriander seeds, toasted and ground

2 pounds Impossible meat

Salt and freshly ground black pepper

FOR THE CASSEROLE

3 red bell peppers

2 eggplants, peeled and sliced into ¼-inch slices

2 teaspoons kosher salt

2 tablespoons canola oil

2 tablespoons Marcona almonds, roughly chopped

> Messa'aa is the Egyptian version of the Greek dish, moussaka.

TO MAKE THE IMPOSSIBLE MESSA'AA

1. Heat the oil in a large cast-iron skillet or Dutch oven over medium-high heat. Add the onion and garlic and cook until translucent.

2. Once the onion and garlic are translucent, add the cardamom, cinnamon, cumin, and coriander seeds and toast. Add the Impossible meat and cook until well browned.

3. Season to taste with salt and pepper and chill completely.

TO MAKE THE CASSEROLE

1. While the Impossible is cooling, roast, peel, and seed the bell peppers. Butterfly the peppers and roast over the stovetop.

2. Lay the eggplant slices in a single layer on a baking sheet that has been lined with paper towels. Sprinkle the eggplant with the salt. Let stand for 1 to 2 hours to draw out all the excess moisture from the eggplant.

3. Preheat the oven to 350°F. Dry the eggplant with a paper towel, lay on an unlined baking sheet, and coat with the canola oil. Roast the eggplant until just cooked through, then remove from the oven and let cool.

4. In a 7-inch square baking pan, layer the Impossible, followed by the bell peppers, then the eggplant, alternating among the three until the pan is filled.

5. Bake for 25 to 30 minutes, or until the casserole is hot all the way through. Let it stand for 5 to 10 minutes before cutting into squares. Finish the plates with the chopped Marcona almonds.

TEARS IN THE RAIN |

BLADE RUNNER (1982)

RICE WHISKEY, CRÈME DE CACAO, BITTERS, CHILI OIL

YIELD: 1 SERVING
GLASSWARE: SHOT GLASS

Meant to be enjoyed along with Deckard when he takes a shot. The float, red in color, mimics the blood that is seen swirling in his glass as he sips.

0.75 ounce unaged rice whiskey

0.75 ounce crème de cacao

1 dropperful (about 1 ml) Peychaud's Chili Oil (recipe follows)

1. Combine the rice whiskey and crème de cacao in an ice-filled mixing glass.

2. Stir and strain into a shot glass.

3. Drop the Peychaud's Chili Oil on top.

PEYCHAUD'S CHILI OIL   YIELD: 15 SERVINGS

¼ ounce Peychaud's Bitters

¼ ounce chili oil

Combine the ingredients in a dropper bottle and shake to mix.

I THINK, THEREFORE I AM

BLADE RUNNER (1982)

ALMOND MILK CUSTARD, ALMOND CRUST, DRIED CHERRIES

YIELD: 4 SERVINGS
ALLERGY: TREE NUTS (ALMOND, WALNUT)
TOOL: FOUR 3-INCH TART TINS

An egg is shown several times in the closing minutes of the film. Taking this imagery but translating it to a vegan dessert, we make an eggless custard.

FOR THE ALMOND CRUST

2 cups almond meal

½ cup white rice flour

3 tablespoons unrefined coconut oil, melted

2 tablespoons honey

FOR THE "CUSTARD FILLING"

1½ cups oat milk

1½ tablespoons agar

1 cup coconut milk

½ cup sugar

3 tablespoons vanilla extract

⅛ teaspoon ground turmeric

FOR THE TOPPING

½ cup chopped walnuts

½ cup dried cherries

½ cup golden raisins

1 tablespoon almond meal

1 tablespoon rum

TO MAKE THE ALMOND CRUST

1. Preheat the oven to 350°F.

2. Mix together all the crust ingredients in a bowl until a dough forms.

3. Press the dough evenly into four 3-inch tart tins and bake for 10 to 12 minutes, until golden

4. Remove from the oven and allow to cool.

TO MAKE THE "CUSTARD FILLING"

1. Combine all the filling ingredients in a medium saucepan and slowly bring to 185°F.

2. While still hot, evenly divide among the baked tart crusts.

3. Cover with plastic wrap and let cool completely.

TO MAKE THE TOPPING

1. Mix all the topping ingredients together in a small bowl and set aside until ready to serve.

2. Top each tart with one-quarter of the topping.

Agar is obtained from various kinds of red seaweed and is used as a thickener in many vegan desserts.

JURASSIC PARK

FEEDING THEM

HE'S A DIGGER

WHERE'S THE GOAT?

CLEVER GIRL

WE GOT DODSON HERE

DINO DNA

CLEVER GIRL | *JURASSIC PARK (1993)*

VODKA, SUZE, CUCUMBER-PEPPERCORN SYRUP, LIME, CELERY BITTERS, DILL

YIELD: 1 SERVING
GLASSWARE: ROCKS GLASS

Who is the hunter and who is the hunted? Robert Muldoon, the park's game warden, thinks that he has outsmarted the mighty Velociraptor, but he soon realizes that she's a . . .

1.75 ounces Żubrówka Bison Grass Vodka

0.5 ounce Cucumber-Peppercorn Syrup (recipe follows)

0.25 ounce Suze Gentian Liqueur

0.5 ounce fresh lime juice

Pinch of salt

1 dash celery bitters

Dill sprig for garnish

1. Combine all the ingredients, except the dill, in a mixing tin, add ice, and shake vigorously.

2. Fine strain into a rocks glass with fresh ice.

3. Garnish with a slapped and expressed dill sprig.

CUCUMBER-PEPPERCORN SYRUP YIELD: 20 SERVINGS

3 English cucumbers

8 cups sugar

2 quarts water

1 ounce pink peppercorns + 1 ounce black peppercorns, coarsely ground

1. Peel the cucumbers and cut through the middle lengthwise. With a spoon, scrape and remove the cucumber seeds (they are extremely bitter) and discard. Roughly dice the peeled, seedless cucumbers and place 4 cups of the diced cucumber in a large bowl.

2. Add the sugar, stir to incorporate with the cucumber, and chill in the fridge for at least 2 hours, preferably overnight.

3. Bring the water to a boil in a large saucepot. Add the cucumber mixture and the peppercorns and cook for 10 minutes. Turn off the heat, allow to cool, and strain.

FEEDING THEM | *JURASSIC PARK (1993)*

PICADILLO, GREEN BEANS, CHAYOTE, GRILLED CORN, SWEET PEPPERS, RICE PILAF

YIELD: 4 SERVINGS

Inspired by the scene where a cow was being fed to the Velociraptors, the dish itself is a common dish you'd find in Central American countries, such as Costa Rica, where the park is located.

FOR THE PICADILLO

2 tablespoons olive oil

2 cups finely chopped
  yellow onion

6 garlic cloves, minced

3 bay leaves

1 pound ground beef and/
  or ground pork

⅓ cup dry white wine

½ cup chicken or beef stock

⅓ cup tomato paste

1 chayote, small diced

½ cup small-diced green beans

½ cup corn

1 red bell pepper, small
  diced and seeded

2 teaspoons dried oregano

2 teaspoon ground cumin

¼ teaspoon cayenne
  pepper (optional)

Salt and freshly ground
  black pepper

FOR THE RICE PILAF

1 cup uncooked long-grain rice

1 tablespoon extra
  virgin olive oil

½ medium yellow onion, diced

1¾ cups vegetable or
  chicken stock or water

½ teaspoon kosher salt

2 tablespoons chopped
  fresh cilantro

TO MAKE THE PICADILLO

1. Heat the oil in the skillet over medium-high heat. Add the onion, garlic and bay leaves, and sauté, stirring frequently, until the onion is soft, about 4 minutes.

2. Add the ground meat and cook until browned. Once the meat is browned, carefully (away from the flame) tilt the pan and remove the excess fat with a large spoon.

3. Add the white wine and stock and cook, stirring, for another minute. Then, add the tomato paste, chayote, green beans, corn, bell pepper, oregano, cumin and cayenne, if using. Simmer over low heat for another 8 minutes, stirring occasionally. Season with salt and pepper to taste.

TO MAKE THE RICE PILAF

1. Place the rice in a strainer and rinse it thoroughly under cool water until the water is only slightly cloudy. There is no need to dry the rice before cooking. Set aside while you cook the onion.

2. Heat the olive oil in a 2-quart saucepan over medium heat. Add the onion and cook until it is translucent and soft.

3. Add the rice to the pot and stir to coat with olive oil. Continue to cook, stirring often, until the tips of the rice turn translucent and the rice smells fragrant and toasted.

4. Pour the stock or water into the saucepan, add the salt, and increase the heat to medium-high. Bring to a boil.

5. As soon as the water comes to a boil, lower the heat to low and cover the pot. Cook without lifting the lid for 15 to 18 minutes. At the end, check that the rice is tender and has absorbed all the liquid. If not, cover and cook for few more minutes, adding a few tablespoons of water, if needed.

6. Remove the pot from heat and let it sit, covered, for another 5 to 10 minutes.

7. Remove the lid and fluff the pilaf with a fork. Transfer to a serving bowl, mix in the cilantro, and serve.

HE'S A DIGGER | *JURASSIC PARK (1993)*

ROASTED BONE MARROW, GRILLED SOURDOUGH, HORSERADISH "SAND"

YIELD: 4 SERVINGS
ALLERGIES: DAIRY (OR CHOOSE DAIRY-FREE BREAD CRUMBS), GLUTEN
TOOL: FOOD PROCESSOR

Working with bone marrow isn't as intimidating as Dr. Grant and his raptor claw.

---

8 ounces panko bread crumbs

One 2-inch piece fresh horseradish, peeled and shredded

¼ cup flat-leaf parsley, chopped

¼ cup vegetable oil

2 marrow bones, split

1 sourdough boule, cut into quarters and sliced

Maldon sea salt

1. Preheat the oven to 300°F and line a baking sheet with parchment paper.

2. Combine the panko, horseradish, and parsley in a food processor and blend until the mixture is sandy in texture. Spread the horseradish "sand" on the prepared baking sheet and place in the oven to dry out for 5 minutes.

3. Heat a grill or a grill pan over medium-high heat until smoking. Brush with a paper towel soaked in the vegetable oil. Brush the remaining oil on the sliced boule and grill to get some grill marks and until the bread gets a little smoky.

4. Preheat the oven to 450°F and line a baking sheet with foil.

5. Place the split marrow bones, cut side up, on the foil-lined baking sheet. Roast for 15 to 20 minutes, or until the marrow is warm in the middle.

6. Remove from the oven and place the cut side of a bone onto a piece of toasted boule, spread the bottom of the plate with the horseradish "sand," and place the bone and bread on top.

> Bone marrow and gremolata is a very classic combination; we gave it a little Nitehawk spin by adding the fresh horseradish.

DINO DNA | *JURASSIC PARK (1993)*

RYE WHISKEY, PUNT E MES, CHILI OIL, SERRANO CHILE, BITTERS

YIELD: 1 SERVING
GLASSWARE: CHILLED ROCKS GLASS (NO ICE)

One of the many rides within Jurassic Park, it's here that we discover the science behind dinosaur cloning. But like this smoky Sazerac variation, the elixir found within this syringe is more dangerous, or in this case, delicious than it seems . . .

1.5 ounces High West Double Rye

0.75 ounce Punt e Mes

3 dashes Double Chili Peychaud's Bitters (recipe follows)

1. Combine all the ingredients in a mixing glass, fill with ice, and stir for 10 seconds.
2. Strain into a chilled rocks glass or syringe.

DOUBLE CHILI PEYCHAUD'S BITTERS YIELD: 10 TO 15 SERVINGS

3 ounces Peychaud's Bitters

0.5 ounce chili oil

1 dried serrano chile, broken up

1. Combine all the ingredients in a glass container and allow to infuse to taste for no more than 1 hour.
2. Fine strain the mixture into a clean jar and store in a cool, dark place.

Stanley Kubrick, who had originally been attached to direct and produce *A.I.*, didn't think special effects had caught up to his vision for the film. Upon seeing *Jurassic Park*, he immediately went back to work on it but passed away before he could do it. The film was ultimately directed by Steven Spielberg.

WE GOT DODSON HERE

JURASSIC PARK (1993)

SPARKLING WINE, MANGO, GUANABANA, LIME, RUM (OPTIONAL)

YIELD: 1 SERVING
GLASSWARE: ROCKS GLASS
TOOLS: ICE POP MOLDS AND
WOODEN ICE POP STICKS

A Costa Rican–themed Champagne cocktail, if you will. Something that Dennis Nedry might drink while waiting for a shaving cream canister from a duplicitous source . . .

---

1 Fruits of Passion Ice Pop
(recipe follows) for garnish

1 ounce white rum (optional)

1 Fruits of Passion Ice Pop
(recipe follows) for garnish

4 ounces cheap sparkling wine
(the cheaper, the better!)

Add Fruits of Passion Ice Pop and rum, if using, to a rocks glass, top with sparkling wine, and enjoy.

FRUITS OF PASSION ICE POP   YIELD: 4 TO 6 SERVINGS

1¼ cups mango juice (Goya
brand recommended)

1¼ cups guanabana juice
(Goya brand recommended)

2 tablespoons fresh lime juice

¼ cup simple syrup

1. Combine all the ice pop ingredients in a large measuring cup or plastic quart container and then fill the ice pop molds three-quarters full with the mixture.

2. Top the mold with its cover, insert wooden ice pop sticks through the holes, and freeze for at least 12 hours.

WHERE'S THE GOAT? | *JURASSIC PARK* (1993)

CURRIED GOAT MOFONGO, SCOTCH BONNET PEPPER, PLANTAIN

YIELD: 4 SERVINGS
TOOLS: SPICE GRINDER, DEEP SAUCEPAN OR DEEP FRYER, MORTAR AND PESTLE, PRESSURE COOKER

The flavors from this dish come from the Caribbean region. The main ingredient comes from the goat that was eaten by the T-Rex. RIP.

FOR THE CURRY BLEND

2 tablespoons whole cumin seeds, toasted

2 tablespoons whole cardamom seeds, toasted

2 tablespoons whole coriander seeds, toasted

¼ cup ground turmeric

1 tablespoon dry mustard

1 teaspoon cayenne pepper

FOR THE MOFONGO

4 plantains

2 cups canola oil

7 garlic cloves, peeled

Salt

2 tablespoon extra virgin olive oil

1 slice bacon, cooked

1 cup chicken stock

FOR THE CURRIED GOAT

2 pounds goat meat

1 teaspoon ground allspice

1 teaspoon kosher salt

3 tablespoons minced garlic

2 tablespoons finely grated fresh ginger

3 tablespoons olive oil

3 scallions, sliced

½ Scotch bonnet pepper, minced (optional)

Fresh cilantro for garnish

TO MAKE THE CURRY BLEND

Grind all the curry blend ingredients in a spice grinder.

TO MAKE THE MOFONGO

1. Peel the plantains and cut into 1-inch slices.

2. Heat the canola oil to 350°F in a deep saucepan or deep fryer. Add the plantain slices in two batches and fry for 7 minutes, turning once, until light golden. Drain on paper towels.

3. Place the garlic in a large mortar or bowl and crush with a pestle or spoon, then sprinkle with salt. Add the olive oil and keep crushing until it's well incorporated.

4. In the same mortar or bowl, crush the fried plantains and cooked bacon into the garlic mixture. Add up to 1 cup of chicken stock as needed to make it moist.

TO MAKE THE CURRIED GOAT

1. Place the goat meat, allspice, salt, 1 tablespoon of the garlic, 1 tablespoon of the ginger, and 3 cups of water in a pressure cooker. Cook at high pressure for 20 minutes.

2. Combine the oil, 2 tablespoons of the curry blend, remaining 2 tablespoons of garlic, and the remaining tablespoon of ginger in a large pot. Cook over low heat until these ingredients combine together into a paste, 3 to 5 minutes. Add the scallions and Scotch bonnet. Let simmer for 2 to 3 minutes.

3. Add the goat and cooking liquid to the curry paste. Add more water if needed, and simmer until tender, 45 to 60 minutes.

TO ASSEMBLE

Scoop mofongo onto a plate or bowl and cover with the curried goat. Garnish with cilantro.

CASABLANCA

A BEAUTIFUL FRIENDSHIP

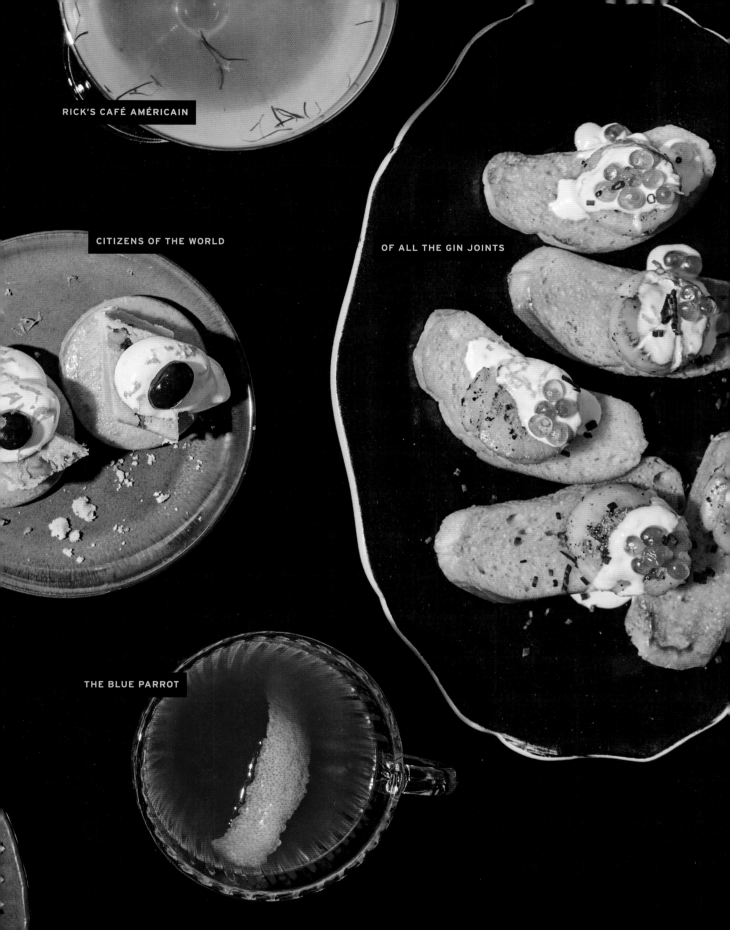

RICK'S CAFÉ AMÉRICAIN

CITIZENS OF THE WORLD

OF ALL THE GIN JOINTS

THE BLUE PARROT

RICK'S CAFÉ AMÉRICAIN |

CASABLANCA (1942)

GIN, CHAMPAGNE, PRESERVED SYRUP, LEMON, SAFFRON

YIELD: 1 SERVING
GLASSWARE: COUPE GLASS

Many French 75 cocktails are enjoyed in Rick's gin joint. This version draws some inspiration from the flavors of Morocco.

1 ounce gin

2 ounces Champagne

0.5 ounce Preserved Lemon Syrup (recipe follows)

0.5 ounce fresh lemon juice

Pinch of saffron for garnish

1. Combine all the ingredients, except the saffron, in an ice-filled mixing glass.
2. Stir and strain into a chilled coupe glass.
3. Garnish with a tiny pinch of saffron.

PRESERVED LEMON SYRUP **YIELD:** 1 CUP

1 cup preserved lemon brine

1 cup sugar

1. Combine all the ingredients in a small, nonreactive saucepan.
2. Bring to a gentle boil.
3. Remove from the heat and allow to cool completely.

For our Nitehawk event, we partnered with Sahadi's, the iconic Middle Eastern grocery. Sahadi's has been a fixture in New York since 1898, and it's been in its original historic storefront on Atlantic Avenue in Brooklyn for more than 50 years.

Like most film stars, Bogart seemed larger than life, but in person he stood 5 feet 8 inches tall. Bergman, however, was almost 2 inches taller. As a result, director Michael Curtiz had Bogie stand on blocks or sit on cushions to make him seem taller than Bergman.

OF ALL THE GIN JOINTS

CASABLANCA (1942)

SEARED SEA SCALLOPS, CHAMPAGNE CRÈME FRAÎCHE, TROUT ROE, BRIOCHE CROSTINI, CHIVES

YIELD: 4 SERVINGS
ALLERGIES: DAIRY, EGG (CHECK BRIOCHE LABEL), FISH, GLUTEN, SHELLFISH

The flavors of the oceanside Casablanca are blended with haute French cuisine. Here you will taste Champagne and caviar and forget about the war.

FOR THE CHAMPAGNE CRÈME FRAÎCHE

1 cup crème fraîche

2 tablespoons Champagne

½ teaspoon salt

⅛ teaspoon lemon zest

FOR THE BRIOCHE CROSTINI

2 small brioche buns

½ pound (2 sticks) unsalted butter, melted

FOR THE SCALLOPS

2 tablespoons canola oil

20 to 30 bay scallops

Salt and freshly ground black pepper

0.5 ounce caviar

1 tablespoon chopped chives

> Ninety-five percent of the caviar produced in the world comes from the Caspian Sea.

TO MAKE THE CHAMPAGNE CRÈME FRAÎCHE

Fold all the ingredients together in a small bowl, transfer to a pastry bag with your desired tip, and refrigerate until just before serving.

TO MAKE THE BRIOCHE CROSTINI

1. Preheat the oven to 200°F.

2. Using a bread knife, thinly slice the brioche into ⅛-inch slices.

3. Brush the slices with the melted butter.

4. Place on a baking sheet and bake for 12 minutes, or until golden brown.

TO MAKE THE SCALLOPS

1. Heat the oil in a large skillet over high heat until nearly smoking.

2. Lightly season the scallops with a small amount of salt and pepper and carefully place in a single layer in the skillet.

3. Cook each side until golden brown, about 90 seconds per side. Remove from the heat.

4. Place a cooked scallop on each crostini.

5. Top each with crème fraiche, caviar, and chives, in that order.

THE BLUE PARROT | *CASABLANCA* (1942)

BOURBON, POMEGRANATE MOLASSES, FIG PRESERVES, MOROCCAN MINT TEA

YIELD: 1 SERVING
GLASSWARE: LARGE TEACUP

Maghrebi mint tea, central to Moroccan life, is spiked here with Rick's drink of choice—Wild Turkey—and other local flavors.

2 ounces Wild Turkey Bourbon

0.5 ounce pomegranate
  molasses

1 ounce fig preserves

Freshly brewed
  Moroccan mint tea

Lemon peel for garnish

1. Combine the bourbon, molasses, and preserves in a large teacup.

2. Top with piping hot Moroccan mint tea.

3. Stir and garnish with a lemon peel.

At the time *Casablanca* was made, censors used a heavy hand when it came to Hollywood films. "I remember after a long time, we could finally say 'hell.' But it had to be a sparse use of 'hell,'" coscreenwriter Julius Epstein recalled. "So, what we would do was write fifty 'hells' and then bargain with them. We'd say, 'How about twenty-five?' We'd wind up with two or three."

A BEAUTIFUL FRIENDSHIP

CASABLANCA (1942)

LAMB TAGINE, MOROCCAN COUSCOUS, GOLDEN RAISINS, FRIED CHICKPEAS, OLIVES, SAFFRON

YIELD: 4 SERVINGS
ALLERGIES: DAIRY, GLUTEN, TREE NUTS (ALMOND)
TOOL: TAGINE OR DUTCH OVEN

The taste and smell of a tagine will instantly bring you to a Moroccan market. In this dish, the lamb, spices, and couscous make a beautiful friendship themselves.

FOR THE LAMB TAGINE

4 pounds boneless lamb, cut into 1-inch pieces
Kosher salt
1 tablespoon olive oil
1 cup chopped onion
4 garlic cloves, chopped
2 teaspoons freshly minced fresh ginger
1 cinnamon stick
½ teaspoon ground turmeric
½ teaspoon ground coriander
¼ teaspoon ground cardamom
¼ teaspoon ground cloves
2 tablespoons tomato paste
Pinch of saffron
3 cups chicken stock
1 cup golden raisins
½ cup sliced Castelvetrano olives

FOR THE MOROCCAN COUSCOUS

2 tablespoons unsalted butter
¼ cup chopped shallot
1 teaspoon kosher salt
½ teaspoon freshly ground black pepper
½ teaspoon ground cumin
2 cups chicken stock
1 cup whole wheat couscous
¼ cup chopped fresh parsley
½ cup toasted almond slivers
2 tablespoons fresh lemon juice
1 tablespoon orange zest
1 tablespoon olive oil

TO MAKE THE LAMB TAGINE

1. Liberally salt the lamb and set aside.
2. Heat the oil in a tagine or Dutch oven.
3. Add the lamb and cook until browned on all sides.
4. Remove the lamb from the pot and set aside.
5. Add the onion, garlic, ginger, cinnamon stock, turmeric, coriander, cardamom, and cloves to the oil and lamb fat. Cook until the garlic starts to brown.
6. Add the tomato paste and stir to combine.
7. Add the saffron and chicken stock, bring to a boil, then lower the heat to a simmer.
8. Return the lamb to the pot and add the raisins and olives.
9. Cover and cook until thickened and the lamb is tender, about 1½ hours.

TO MAKE THE MOROCCAN COUSCOUS

1. Melt the butter over medium heat in a pot that has a lid.
2. Add the shallot and let brown.
3. Add the salt, pepper, cumin, and stock and bring to a boil.
4. Remove from the heat and stir in the couscous.
5. Cover the pot with its lid and let stand for 5 minutes.
6. Stir in the parsley, toasted almonds, lemon juice, orange zest, and olive oil.

> Saffron is the most expensive food by weight in the world.

WE'LL ALWAYS HAVE PARIS

CASABLANCA (1942)

COGNAC, TURKISH COFFEE, CARDAMOM CACAO CREAM, RAS EL HANOUT

YIELD: 1 SERVING
GLASSWARE: IRISH COFFEE GLASS

This could be the beginning of a beautiful friendship.

1.5 ounces cognac
0.5 ounce demerara syrup
6 ounces brewed Turkish coffee
Cardamom Cacao Cream (recipe follows)
Ras el hanout for garnish

1. Combine the cognac, demerara syrup, and piping hot Turkish coffee in an Irish coffee glass.
2. Top with Cardamom Cacao Cream, and dust a pinch of ras el hanout on top.

CARDAMOM CACAO CREAM YIELD: 1 PINT

24 green cardamom pods
¼ cup cacao nibs
1 pint heavy cream

1. Combine all the ingredients in a pot and simmer below a boil for 5 minutes.
2. Remove from the heat, allow to cool completely, and strain.
3. Whip in an iSi charger or mixer, or by shaking by hand in a cocktail shaker tin.

> The release of *Casablanca* was rushed because of real-life world events. Originally the film was slated for release in early 1943, but the film premiered at the Hollywood Theater in New York City on November 26, 1942. Why? The publicity people moved it forward to coincide with the Allied invasion of North Africa and the capture of Casablanca.

CITIZENS OF THE WORLD

CASABLANCA (1942)

FRENCH BUTTER COOKIE, PISTACHIO HALVA, ORANGE CREAM, CHOCOLATE ESPRESSO BEANS

YIELD: 4 SERVINGS
ALLERGIES: DAIRY, GLUTEN, TREE NUTS (PISTACHIO)
TOOL: ROLLING PIN

A marriage of the French and North African cuisines with the classic French cookie filled with pistachios. The orange and coffee flavors contrast and enhance each other.

FOR THE FRENCH BUTTER COOKIES

10 tablespoons unsalted butter

½ cup granulated sugar

1 teaspoon vanilla extract

1 large egg

Scant 2¼ cups all-purpose flour

Scant ½ teaspoon baking powder

Pinch of salt

FOR THE EGG WASH

1 large egg

1 tablespoon heavy cream

FOR THE ORANGE CREAM

1 cup heavy cream

¼ cup confectioners' sugar

Zest of 1 orange

2 tablespoons triple sec

FOR ASSEMBLY

Pistachio halva

Chocolate espresso beans

TO MAKE THE FRENCH BUTTER COOKIES

1. Cream together the butter and granulated sugar in a stand mixer fitted with the paddle attachment until fluffy.

2. Stir together the vanilla and egg in a small bowl, then slowly mix into the butter mixture.

3. Stir together the flour, baking powder, and salt in another bowl, then slowly add to the butter mixture, mixing until just combined. Do not overmix.

4. Refrigerate for 45 minutes, then roll out to ¼-inch thickness.

5. Lie dough flat on a baking sheet and refrigerate overnight.

6. With a 2-inch ring mold, cut disks from the cold dough. Refrigerate the cookies again on their baking sheet.

TO MAKE THE EGG WASH AND BAKE THE COOKIES

1. Preheat the oven to 350°F.

2. Meanwhile, whisk together the egg and cream in a small bowl.

3. Before putting in the oven, brush all the chilled cookie disks with egg wash.

4. Bake for 12 minutes, or until golden brown. Remove from the oven and let cool.

TO MAKE THE ORANGE CREAM

1. Whisk together the cream and confectioners' sugar in a small bowl until firm.

2. Fold in the orange zest and triple sec.

TO ASSEMBLE

Layer the butter cookies with the halva and a dollop of orange cream. Top each dollop with an espresso bean.

MIDNITE MOVIES:

BEST CONSUMED PAST THE WITCHING HOUR

The Midnite Movie is more than just a film; it's a magical, shared experience in the cinema late at night, when the weird, wild, and wacky dazzle audiences who stay up way past the witching hour. Rising up from the underground circuit and influenced by late-night tales of terror on television, the Midnite Movie flourished when it found a permanent home in downtown New York City in the 1970s.

The combination of such brave filmmakers as John Waters and David Lynch; a group of theaters like the Elgin, St. Marks, the Waverly, and the 8th Street Playhouse; and a daring audience came together to create this completely new form of moviegoing. Eventually, this movement spread nationwide and inspired the next wave of late-night auteurs who continue to defy convention.

B-YATCH-CH | *US* (2019)

RABBIT MEATBALLS, CALABRIAN CHILI PASTE, RED WINE SAUCE, PARSLEY, GRILLED BAGUETTE

YIELD: 4 SERVINGS
ALLERGIES: DAIRY, GLUTEN

B-Yacht-ch is the name of one of the boats in the marina that Elisabeth Moss's character is seen on. Ominous rabbits are featured throughout the movie, and Jordan Peele has spoken about how he is terrified of them!

FOR THE MEATBALLS

2 garlic cloves, minced

1 shallot, minced

1 teaspoon fresh
   rosemary, minced

1 teaspoon fresh thyme

½ pound (2 sticks)
   unsalted butter

1½ cups heavy cream

2 cups diced challah bread

1 pound ground rabbit

1 pound ground chicken thigh

4 teaspoons salt

One 0.25-ounce packet
   powdered gelatin

3 tablespoons Calabrian
   chili paste

FOR THE SAUCE

2 tablespoons extra
   virgin olive oil

⅛ cup large-diced carrot

⅛ cup large-diced
   Spanish onion

3½ tablespoons tomato paste

1 cup red wine

1 sprig rosemary

1 sprig thyme

½ pound veal demi-glace

1 cup water

FOR ASSEMBLY
AND SERVING

2 tablespoons extra
   virgin olive oil

Toasted baguette, two
   slices per serving

Fresh parsley for garnish

TO MAKE THE MEATBALLS

1. Sweat the garlic, shallot, rosemary, and thyme in the butter in a medium frying pan over medium-high heat.

2. Once you can start to smell the herbs, add 1 cup of the cream and bring to a boil.

3. Add the diced bread and cook until the bread has absorbed all the liquid.

4. Remove from the heat and let cool completely.

5. Combine the ground rabbit, ground chicken, salt, and powdered gelatin in a stand mixer fitted with the paddle attachment. Beat on low speed until well mixed.

6. Add the panade (bread mixture) and mix on medium speed until well combined.

7. Slowly drizzle in the remaining ½ cup of cream while beating on low speed.

8. Remove half of the mixture and mix the Calabrian chili paste into the other half.

TO MAKE THE SAUCE

1. Heat the oil in a large pot until smoking, then add and brown the carrots, onion, and tomato paste.

2. Deglaze with red wine and reduce until the alcohol has cooked off. Add the sprig of rosemary and sprig of thyme. Add the veal demi-glace and water, bring to a boil, and then allow the sauce to reduce to desired consistency. Remove the sprigs of rosemary and thyme upon finishing.

CONTINUED ▶

> Panade is a base that adds fat to and binds lean meats that are being used in meatballs or sausages.

TO ASSEMBLE AND SERVE

1. Heat the oil in a large frying pan.

2. Form each meatball mixture into 1-inch balls.

3. Cook the meatballs, turning frequently, until browned and they have an internal temperature of 155°F.

4. Serve two regular balls and two spicy balls in each bowl, topped with the sauce.

5. Finish with a toasted baguette and chopped parsley.

Director Jordan Peele has said that the inspiration for *Us* came in part from *The Twilight Zone* TV show episode "Mirror Image," was centered on a young woman and her evil doppelgänger.

9/11 TRIBUTE SHOT | *JENNIFER'S BODY (2009)*

RED, WHITE, AND BLUE ORANGE-GIN SHOT

YIELD: 1 SERVING
GLASSWARE: TALL, CLEAR
SHOT GLASS

This is a layered red, white, and blue shot as seen in the movie. The classic version of this is made with grenadine, crème de cacao, and blue curaçao. Our version is less cloyingly sweet and more balanced. It also uses fresher ingredients, including a delicious house-made grenadine.

0.5 ounce House-Made Grenadine (recipe follows)
0.25 ounce fresh lemon juice
0.25 ounce Solerno Blood Orange Liqueur
0.5 ounce Empress 1908 Gin

1. Pour the grenadine into a tall, clear shot glass.
2. Mix together the lemon juice and blood orange liqueur in a small container.
3. Slowly pour the lemon juice mixture on top of the grenadine, using an inverted spoon to slow the force of the pour.
4. Slowly pour the gin on top, again using an inverted spoon to slow the pour. The ingredients should form three distinct layers: red, white, and blue.

HOUSE-MADE GRENADINE   YIELD: ABOUT 1 CUP

1 cup pomegranate juice
1 cup + 2 tablespoons sugar
2 tablespoons pomegranate molasses
¼ teaspoon orange blossom water

1. Combine all the ingredients, except the orange blossom water, in a small saucepan and cook over medium-high heat for 10 minutes, stirring occasionally.
2. Remove from the heat and allow to cool for at least 10 minutes. Add the orange blossom water.

CONTINUED ▶

Grenadine is a commonly used, nonalcoholic bar syrup characterized by a flavor that is both tart and sweet, and by a deep red color. It is popular as an ingredient in cocktails, both for its flavor and to give a reddish or pink tint to mixed drinks, and is traditionally made from pomegranate.

The title of the film is a reference to the Hole song of the same name. The Hole song "Violet" is also featured in *Jennifer's Body*.

VIOLET BLUE DRAGON MANDOO

OLDBOY (2003)

FRIED PORK AND KIMCHI DUMPLINGS, GOCHUGARU DIPPING SAUCE

YIELD: MAKES 10 SERVINGS
ALLERGIES: GLUTEN, SOY

In the 15 years that Oh Dae-Su is imprisoned, he is fed endless amounts of fried dumplings, the taste of which end up being a key to finding his captors once released. These are a classic Korean *mandoo*, deep-fried and crispy in the style of Violet Blue Dragon, the Chinese restaurant featured in the movie.

FOR THE DUMPLINGS

1 ounce dried dangmyeon (Korean glass noodles)
½ cup packed bean sprouts
½ cup kimchi, drained and minced
3 tablespoons drained and crumbled tofu
4 scallions
1 pound ground pork
1 teaspoon salt
¼ teaspoon ground white pepper
50 dumpling wrappers (glutinous preferred)

FOR THE DIPPING SAUCE

1 teaspoon gochugaru (Korean red pepper powder)
¼ cup soy sauce
¼ cup rice vinegar
1 tablespoon sesame oil
Juice of ½ lime

FOR ASSEMBLY

Vegetable oil for deep-frying
Shredded scallions

TO MAKE THE DUMPLINGS

1. Cook the dangmyeon in boiling water for 6 minutes. Remove and rinse in cold water. Chop into small pieces.

2. Cook the bean sprouts in boiling water for about 30 seconds. Remove and rinse in cold water. Chop into small pieces.

3. Mix together the noodles, bean sprouts, and all the remaining dumpling ingredients, except the wrappers, in a large bowl until well combined.

4. Place about 1 tablespoon of filling in each dumpling wrapper. Wet the edges of the wrapper, fold in half, and pleat the edges to seal. Repeat with the remaining filling and wrappers.

5. The dumplings can be frozen on a tray or plate in a single layer. Once frozen, they can be stored in a freezer bag or freezer-safe container until ready to cook.

TO MAKE THE DIPPING SAUCE

Mix together all the ingredients in a small, nonreactive bowl.

TO ASSEMBLE

1. Working in batches, deep-fry dumplings in a large pot or deep fryer over medium heat until golden brown and crispy, 3 to 4 minutes per batch.

2. Top with shredded scallions and serve with the dipping sauce.

CONTINUED ▶

Four octopuses were eaten for this classic scene in *Oldboy* with Dae-su (Choi Min-sik) in the sushi bar. Director Chan-wook Park thanked the octopuses along with the cast and crew when the film won the Grand Prix at Cannes.

EL TOPO | *EL TOPO* (1970)

MEZCAL, HONEY SYRUP, LIME, MOLE BITTERS

YIELD: 1 SERVING
GLASSWARE: COUPE GLASS

El Topo is Spanish for "The Mole," a Mexican-inspired cocktail with mole bitters (a translational pun) and honey, a nod to the symbolism of the bees in the film.

1.5 ounces mezcal

0.75 ounce Honey Syrup (recipe follows)

0.5 ounce fresh lime juice

3 dashes mole or Aztec bitters

Nutmeg for garnish

1. Combine all the ingredients, except the garnish, in an ice-filled mixing glass.

2. Stir and strain into a coupe glass.

3. Garnish with freshly grated nutmeg.

HONEY SYRUP YIELD: ABOUT 1½ CUPS

1 cup honey

1 cup water

1. Combine the honey and water in a small saucepot and bring to a low boil.

2. Remove from the heat and allow to cool completely.

CONTINUED ▶

Among all the fans of *El Topo*, including David Lynch, Bob Dylan, and Dennis Hopper, it was John Lennon who urged his lawyer, Allen Klein, to purchase the distribution rights that Klein's company, ABKCO, owns to this day.

THEY'RE COMING TO GET YOU, BARBRA | *NIGHT OF THE LIVING DEAD (1968)*

SCOTCH, DON'S MIX, VELVET FALERNUM, LIME, RUM, MORE RUM, BECHEROVKA, BITTERS, MINT

YIELD: 1 SERVING
ALLERGY: TREE NUTS (ALMOND)
GLASSWARE: COLLINS OR TIKI GLASS

A literal Zombie variation to pair with this seminal horror movie. But be forewarned—too many of these and you'll feel like the undead in the morning!

1.5 ounces Black Bottle Blended Scotch Whiskey

0.66 ounce Don's Mix: Grapefruit-Cinnamon Cordial (recipe follows)

0.33 ounce John D. Taylor's Velvet Falernum

0.66 ounces fresh lime juice

0.33 ounce Smith & Cross Traditional Jamaican Rum

0.25 ounce Cruzan Black Strap Rum

0.18 ounce Becherovka

1 heavy dash Angostura Bitters for garnish

Expressed mint crown for garnish

1. Combine all the ingredients, except the garnishes, in a mixing tin. Crack three or four ice cubes with the back of a tablespoon and add all of the shards to the mixing tin.

2. Shake vigorously for 5 seconds, then dump the contents into your glass, topping with cracked ice.

3. Garnish with a heavy dash of bitters and expressed mint crown.

> The iconic soundtrack of *The Night of the Living Dead*, along with the film itself, has influenced decades of subsequent horror films. Our good friends, the Brooklyn band Morricone Youth, who specialize in reimagined soundtracks, performed at Nitehawk's original location in a yearly Halloween tradition that featured a screening of the movie with a unique live soundtrack.

DON'S MIX: GRAPEFRUIT-CINNAMON CORDIAL   YIELD: 10 TO 12 SERVINGS

1 cup grapefruit juice

1 cup demerara sugar

2 to 3 cinnamon sticks, broken

1. Combine all the ingredients in a large pot and bring to a boil. Lower the heat to a low boil and simmer for 15 minutes. Stir and check the flavor as you go.

2. Remove from the heat and leave the cinnamon sticks in the pot as it cools.

3. Fine strain, discarding the cinnamon pieces, and refrigerate.

CONTINUED ▶

For the scene in *Night of the Living Dead* in which Karen Cooper (Kyra Schon) begins eating her father's corpse, the crew's leftover lunch was employed. "Earlier in the day, we were eating hamburgers or meatball sandwiches, so they just smeared chocolate syrup all over it and that's what I was biting into," Schon said.

LEATHERFACE JERKY

THE TEXAS CHAIN SAW MASSACRE (1974)

TEXAS-THAI CHILI, GARLIC, SOY

YIELD: 4 TO 6 SERVINGS
ALLERGIES: FISH (CHOOSE GLUTEN-FREE FISH SAUCE IF NEEDED), SOY

One of the only items that has never left our menu in over 10 years is this jerky. A fan favorite just like this film, best enjoyed before the movie gets too gruesome!

3 garlic cloves

1 Thai chile

1 cup ketchup

½ cup apple cider vinegar

¼ cup honey

1 cup soy sauce

¼ cup mirin

¼ cup rice vinegar

2 ounces fresh ginger, peeled

3 lime leaves (optional)

5 dashes Asian fish sauce

2 pounds flank steak

1. Combine all the ingredients, except the steak, in a 3-quart saucepot and blend with an immersion blender. If you do not have an immersion blender, use a regular blender to blend all of the solids and half of the liquids.

2. Bring the mixture to a boil, then remove from the heat and chill completely. This will be your marinade.

3. While the marinade is chilling, remove and discard any silver skin and excess fat from the flank steak and slice very thinly, going against the grain.

4. Once the marinade is cool, marinate the sliced steak in a resealable plastic bag, making sure the marinade is fully coating each piece of steak. Marinate for a minimum of 4 hours, ideally overnight.

5. Preheat the oven to 180°F. Remove the steak from the marinade and reserve the marinade. Lay out the steak on a wire rack placed on a baking sheet lined with parchment paper.

6. Put the pan into the oven and, after 45 minutes, flip the steak to the second side. Return to the oven and dry out for another 45 minutes, then dip the dried steak into the reserved marinade. Put back into the oven for 10 to 15 minutes, or until the steak is shiny but dry. Let cool at room temperature. Stays good refrigerated for up to 2 weeks.

CONTINUED ▶

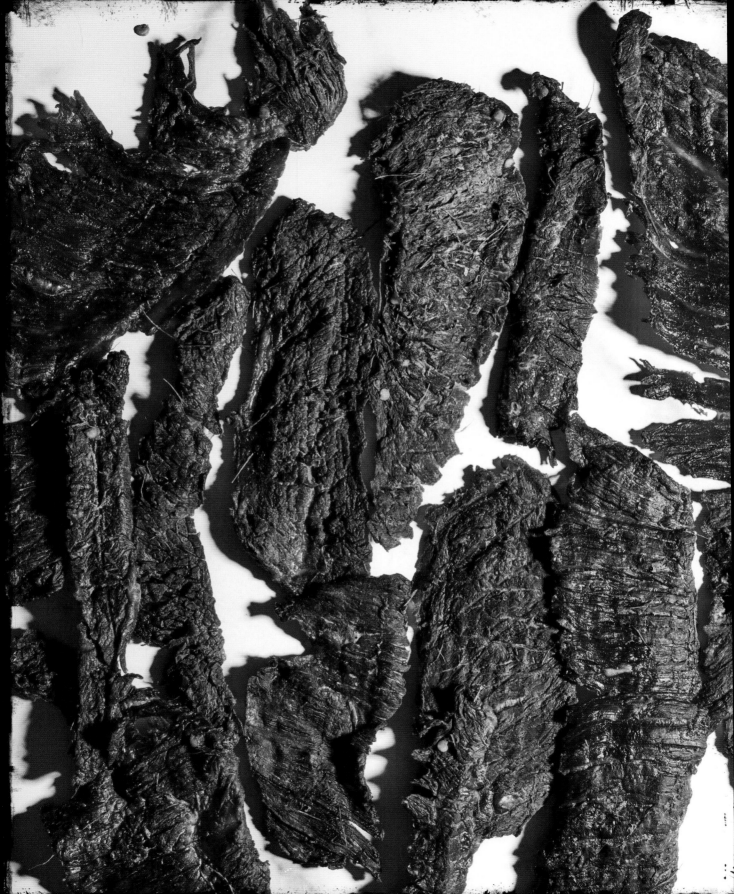

Although originally located in Williamston County, near Austin, Texas, the original home used in the film is restored and now in use as a restaurant called the Grand Central Café located in Kingsland, Texas.

TWIN MOTOR DRIVE | *AKIRA* (1988)

BIG MARTY BUNS, BURGERS, SHIITAKE MUSHROOMS, JAPANESE MAYO, WASABI KETCHUP

YIELD: 4 SERVINGS
ALLERGIES: DAIRY, EGGS, FISH, GLUTEN, SOY
TOOLS: GRILL, FOOD PROCESSOR

The name comes from the motorcycle part that makes Shōtarō Kaneda's (iconic) cycle unique and fast. Having escaped the hospital, Tetsuo (Kaneda's friend and the major antagonist of the film) meets up with his girlfriend and they enjoy a burger together. All before he steals Kaneda's bike. We skid this dish sideways with some of our favorite Japanese condiments, including a wasabi ketchup and a mock-Kewpie mayo.

FOR THE BURGERS

½ cup panko or other dry bread crumbs

¼ cup whole milk

8 ounces ground sirloin

8 ounces ground pork

¼ cup finely chopped white onion

1½ teaspoons soy sauce

½ teaspoon salt

¼ teaspoon freshly ground black pepper

Sesame oil for coating hands

FOR THE JAPANESE MAYONNAISE

1 tablespoon rice vinegar

3½ teaspoons malt vinegar

½ teaspoon kosher salt

¼ teaspoon MSG powder (optional)

¼ teaspoon Japanese mustard powder

Pinch of hon dashi powder (ground bonito flakes)

Small pinch of garlic powder

1 large egg yolk

½ cup vegetable oil

FOR THE WASABI KETCHUP

½ cup ketchup

2 tablespoons soy sauce

1 tablespoon wasabi paste

TO MAKE THE BURGER PATTIES

1. Prepare a grill for medium heat. Combine the bread crumbs and milk in a large bowl and let rest 2 to 3 minutes. Add the sirloin, pork, onion, soy sauce, salt, and pepper. Knead the meat until it becomes sticky and binds together; divide into four parts.

2. Lightly dab your hands with sesame oil. Using your palms, roll each portion of the meat into a ball, then pat the ball flat, shifting it from hand to hand, to form a ½-inch-thick patty. Make a shallow indentation across the center of the patty with the side of your hand to keep it from puffing while it grills.

TO MAKE THE JAPANESE MAYONNAISE

1. Whisk together the rice vinegar, malt vinegar, salt, MSG, mustard powder, hon dashi powder, and garlic powder in a small bowl, until the hon dashi is completely dissolved.

2. Transfer the vinegar mixture to a food processor fitted with a steel blade and add the egg yolk. Pulse to combine.

3. With the motor running, slowly drizzle in the vegetable oil in a thin, steady stream. Transfer the mayonnaise to an airtight container and store in refrigerator for up to 2 weeks.

TO MAKE THE WASABI KETCHUP

Whisk together the ketchup, soy sauce, and wasabi paste in a small bowl.

CONTINUED ▷

FOR THE SAUTÉED MUSHROOMS

1½ **teaspoons olive, canola, or other oil**

2 **tablespoons unsalted butter**

6 **ounces shiitake mushrooms**

½ **teaspoon sea salt, plus more to taste if desired**

½ **teaspoon freshly ground black pepper, or to taste**

3 **garlic cloves, finely chopped**

1 **cup white wine**

FOR ASSEMBLY

4 **potato rolls (Big Marty's Sesame Rolls recommended)**

A salad or fries on the side

TO MAKE THE SAUTÉED MUSHROOMS

1. Heat a heavy pan or cast-iron skillet over medium heat.

2. Add the oil and 1 tablespoon of the butter.

3. When almost smoking, add the mushrooms.

4. Stir and let the mushrooms brown; slightly season with salt and pepper.

5. Add the remaining tablespoon of butter and the garlic. Stir quickly to heat the garlic, but be careful not to let it burn.

6. Add the white wine. (Caution: It will release a LOT of steam when it hits the pan.) Let the wine cook down.

7. When the liquid is fully absorbed, taste. Add any additional salt to taste (don't add before; the butter may make your mushrooms saltier than you realize when cooked down).

TO ASSEMBLE

1. Lightly toast the buns.

2. Spread Japanese mayonnaise on the bottom of each bun.

3. Place a burger on top.

4. Place a spoonful of the mushroom mixture on top of each patty.

5. Spread wasabi ketchup on the underside of each bun top and place on the mushroom mixture.

6. Serve with a salad or fries.

One of the most expensive and highest-grossing Japanese animated features of all time, *Akira* has spawned video games and soundtrack remixes, and become a visual touchstone in pop culture. Since acquiring the rights in 2002, Warner Brothers has planned a live-action remake, which after a few false starts still hasn't happened yet as of today.

DRIVE-THRU MEAL | *DRIVE (2011)*

DOUBLE-DOUBLE, AMERICAN CHEESE, SPECIAL SAUCE, HAND-CUT FRIES

YIELD: 1 SERVING
ALLERGIES: DAIRY, GLUTEN

As truthful of a re-creation of the famous In-N-Out Double-Double that can be found. A movie about driving that takes place in California needs California's best drive-thru burger.

**FOR THE SPECIAL SAUCE
(PER SERVING)**

3 tablespoons mayonnaise

1 tablespoon ketchup

**1 tablespoon dill pickle,
roughly chopped**

1 teaspoon sugar

½ teaspoon white vinegar

⅛ teaspoon salt

**FOR THE BURGERS
(PER SERVING)**

4 ounces ground beef

**FOR ASSEMBLY
(PER SERVING)**

1 potato roll, split

Oil for pan

Salt

2 slices American cheese

One ¼-inch slice white onion

1 butter lettuce leaf

One ¼-inch slice tomato

FOR THE FRIES

1 russet potato per serving

2 quarts water

2 tablespoons white vinegar

2 tablespoons salt

Sunflower oil for frying

TO MAKE THE SPECIAL SAUCE

Mix together all the sauce ingredients in a small bowl and refrigerate until ready to use.

TO MAKE THE BURGERS

1. Divide the ground beef into two 2-ounce patties.

2. Between two pieces of waxed paper, roll out each burger into a 4-inch patty.

TO ASSEMBLE

1. In a lightly oiled skillet large enough to later hold both patties, toast each half of the potato roll over high heat, then set aside.

2. Lightly oil the skillet again and turn down the heat to medium-high.

3. Salt both burgers lightly before putting into the pan.

4. Cook for 2 minutes on one side.

5. Flip. Place a piece of cheese on each burger and put a white onion slice on only one of the two burgers.

6. Cook for 2 minutes and then remove from the heat.

7. Build each burger in this order: bottom bun, Thousand Island sauce, lettuce, tomato, burger with cheese, burger with cheese and onion, top bun.

CONTINUED ▶

> Inspired by the famous West Coast institution, In-N-Out Burger will never open on the East Coast because its owners will not build somewhere greater than 500 miles from their commissaries.

1. Peel and cut the potatoes into ¼-inch batons. Submerge in cold water until ready to use.

2. Bring the 2 quarts of water, vinegar, salt, and potatoes to a boil in a large pot and boil for 10 minutes.

3. Drain the potatoes and completely dry them with paper towels.

4. In a Dutch oven or a heavy-bottomed pot, bring the oil to 400°F.

5. Cook the potatoes in batches for 1 minute per batch, then drain and dry again.

6. When ready to serve, bring the oil back to 400°F and fry the fries until golden and crispy.

According to director Nicolas Winding Refn, due to the fact that it was mostly a night shoot, they lined the collar of Ryan Gosling's Scorpion jacket with silver material so his "beautiful face" would be visible. This film was also one of the first that Nitehawk Cinema played when opening in 2011, and certainly our first big success.

A Dark and Stormy with Goslings Black Seal Rum and Goslings Stormy Ginger Beer will accompany any great Ryan Gosling film.

WONDER WHEEL | *THE WARRIORS (1979)*

CONEY ISLAND–STYLE BROOKLYN BLACKOUT CAKE

YIELD: 4 SERVINGS
ALLERGIES: DAIRY, EGG, GLUTEN
TOOL: SQUEEZE BOTTLE

The classic Brooklyn blackout cake is done up with Coney Island flair. The film's eponymous gang's home turf is Coney Island, Brooklyn, and this decadent cake pays tribute to the amusement park and the iconic Ferris wheel that made it famous.

FOR THE CHOCOLATE FUNNEL CAKE

1 large egg

¼ cup granulated sugar

1¾ cups + 4 teaspoons milk

1 teaspoon vanilla extract

1⅓ cups + 1 tablespoon all-purpose flour, sifted

¼ teaspoon salt

2 tablespoons dark cocoa powder

Enough canola oil for a 1-inch depth in pan

FOR THE CHOCOLATE PUDDING

⅓ cup granulated sugar

½ cup dark cocoa powder

2½ tablespoons cornstarch

¼ teaspoon salt

3⅔ cups milk

2 large eggs

2 teaspoons vanilla extract

5.5 ounces dark chocolate

3½ tablespoons unsalted butter

FOR THE CHOCOLATE SAUCE

¾ cup + 1 tablespoon milk

7 ounces milk chocolate

3 tablespoons + 1 teaspoon corn syrup

FOR ASSEMBLY

Confectioners' sugar for dusting

TO MAKE THE CHOCOLATE FUNNEL CAKE

1. Whisk together the egg, sugar, milk, and vanilla in a medium bowl.

2. Mix together the flour, salt, and cocoa in a large bowl.

3. Add the milk mixture to the flour mixture and whisk together until just combined.

4. Transfer the batter to a squeeze bottle.

5. Pour the oil to a 1-inch depth in a deep skillet or saucepan and heat to 350°F.

6. Swirl in the batter to form a 3-inch circle.

7. Halfway through cooking, when the underside has crisped, flip the funnel cake.

8. Remove from the oil and dry on a paper towel. Continue until all the batter is cooked.

TO MAKE THE CHOCOLATE PUDDING

1. Combine the sugar, cocoa powder, cornstarch, and salt in a large saucepan.

2. Whisk together the milk, eggs, and vanilla in a medium bowl.

3. Add the milk mixture to the pot and heat over medium heat.

4. While the mixture heats, slowly whisk in the dark chocolate until melted.

5. Cook at a simmer for 3 minutes.

6. Remove from the heat and whisk in the butter.

7. Lay plastic wrap across the top of the warm pudding and allow to fully cool.

CONTINUED ▶

TO MAKE THE CHOCOLATE SAUCE

1. Bring the milk to a boil in a small saucepan and turn off the heat.

2. Place the chocolate and corn syrup in a heatproof bowl, add the milk mixture, and whisk until combined.

3. Allow to cool.

TO ASSEMBLE

1. Place one funnel cake on a plate.

2. Scoop and lightly spread some pudding on top.

3. Top with another funnel cake.

4. Scoop and lightly spread some pudding on top.

5. Place a third funnel cake on top.

6. Dust with confectioners' sugar.

7. Finish with chocolate sauce.

The actors all had to remove their Warriors vests between takes, as the producers feared they'd be mistaken for actual gang members by real gangs in the city.

SPLITTING THE SHORES |

UNDER THE SKIN (2013)

SCOTCH, SWEET VERMOUTH, AMARETTO, ROOT BEER, BITTERS

YIELD: 1 SERVING
GLASSWARE: ROCKS GLASS

This cocktail is as gorgeous as the Scottish shore.

1.5 ounces Scotch
0.75 ounce sweet vermouth
0.5 ounce amaretto
0.25 ounce root beer liqueur
3 dashes Angostura Bitters
Orange peel for garnish

1. Combine all the ingredients, except the garnish, in an ice-filled mixing glass. Stir and strain into an ice-filled rocks glass.

2. Garnish with an orange peel.

The majority of the cast are nonactors, and much of the film was shot with hidden cameras without the participants' knowledge beforehand.

OOZE | *UNDER THE SKIN (2013)*

BLACK BEAN SOUP, AVOCADO PUREE, CHICHARRONES

YIELD: 4 TO 6 SERVINGS
ALLERGY: SHELLFISH

You'll be dragged into the black world (or void) with this black bean soup reflective of the black liquid abyss.

FOR THE SOUP

2 tablespoons canola oil

2 garlic cloves, minced

½ cup small-diced white onion

1 teaspoon coriander
  seeds, ground

1 teaspoon cumin seeds, ground

¼ teaspoon mustard
  seeds, ground

1 tablespoon black squid ink

Two 24-ounce cans black
  beans, drained and rinsed

4 cups low-sodium
  vegetable stock

Salt

Tabasco or other hot sauce

FOR THE AVOCADO PUREE

2 ripe avocados

Zest and juice of 1 lime

¼ cup extra virgin olive oil

1 teaspoon sriracha

Salt

FOR SERVING

Store-bought chicharrones

TO MAKE THE SOUP

1. Heat the oil in a 3-quart saucepot over medium heat and sweat the minced garlic and onion.

2. Once the onion and garlic are translucent, add the ground coriander, cumin, and mustard seeds and let them toast lightly.

3. Add the squid ink, black beans, and vegetable stock. Bring to a boil, then lower the heat to a simmer.

4. Cook until the beans are tender and almost falling apart.

5. Blend the soup with either an immersion blender or in batches in a blender until smooth. Season with salt and Tabasco. Either keep the soup hot or chill completely; the soup will stay good in the refrigerator for 2 to 3 days.

TO MAKE THE AVOCADO PUREE

1. Make sure the avocados are ripe but not overripe with black spots, as the latter will cause your puree to blacken.

2. Remove the avocado flesh from the skin and, breaking it into medium chunks, place in a blender.

3. Add the lime zest and juice, oil, sriracha, and salt to taste. Blend slowly to combine. Once fully combined, increase the speed to high to incorporate some air into the mixture. Store in a sealed container for 3 to 4 hours with a piece of plastic wrap touching the surface of the puree.

TO SERVE

Serve the soup hot with a spoonful of the avocado puree and crushed store-bought chicharrones.

TENAFLY VIPER | *STREET TRASH (1987)*

BRANDY, LEMON, GRAPE SODA

YIELD: 1 SERVING
GLASSWARE: ONE 200-MILLILITER
BRANDY BOTTLE

A "molten hobo holocaust" set in our very own Williamsburg, Brooklyn, neighborhood during the '80s.

2 ounces E&J Brandy VS
0.5 ounce fresh lemon juice
3 ounces grape soda

1. Combine all the ingredients in an ice-filled mixing glass.
2. Stir and strain into an empty 200-milliliter brandy bottle.

Street Trash was shot almost entirely in Williamsburg, Brooklyn, mere blocks from the first Nite-hawk location. The neighborhood has changed significantly in those 30-plus years.

CHEDDAR GOBLIN | *MANDY (2018)*

SPICY MAC AND CHEESE GRILLED CHEESE, PICKLED JALAPEÑO, SOURDOUGH

YIELD: 4 SERVINGS
ALLERGIES: DAIRY, GLUTEN
TOOL: GRIDDLE PAN (OPTIONAL)

Who doesn't love mac and cheese and grilled cheese? Combine them and you get this fun, rich way to hang out with Nick and the Cheddar Goblin.

FOR THE MAC AND CHEESE

8 ounces jalapeño Velveeta

1 pound Velveeta

2 cups milk

¼ cup pickled jalapeño peppers (see Queso recipe, page 234)

¼ cup sour cream

1 pound macaroni elbows

FOR THE GRILLED CHEESE SANDWICHES

1 sourdough torpedo loaf

8 ounces sliced Muenster

½ cup pickled jalapeño peppers

4 tablespoons (½ stick) unsalted butter

TO MAKE THE MAC AND CHEESE

1. Combine the two Velveetas, milk, pickled jalapeños, and sour cream in a 3-quart saucepot. Over low heat, melt the cheeses, stirring often, making sure not to scorch the milk or cheese.

2. Once melted, blend either with an immersion blender or regular blender.

3. Cook the macaroni according to the package instructions. Drain and combine with the cheese sauce and let cool.

TO MAKE THE GRILLED CHEESE SANDWICHES

1. While the macaroni and cheese cools, slice the bread into ½-inch-thick slices

2. Build the sandwiches with one slice of Muenster, a few pickled jalapeños, and enough mac and cheese to cover the bread.

3. Melt enough butter in a large sauté pan or griddle pan, over medium heat, to cover the bottom of the pan. Place the grilled cheese sandwich in the pan, cook on the first side until the bread is golden brown, flip the sandwich, and cook until the cheese is melted and the mac and cheese is hot.

4. Remove from the pan and let the sandwich, sit for 1 to 2 minutes before slicing.

CONTINUED ▶

The weapon forged by Red is an homage to the letter F in Swiss metal band Celtic Frost's logo. This soundtrack is one for the ages.

The Cheddar Goblin is the terrifying mascot for a fictional brand of mac and cheese in *Mandy*. In the ad, we see the goblin emerge from a bowl of macaroni to vomit cheesy pasta all over a pair of smiling children.

VOLK SUSPIRIA | *SUSPIRIA (2018)*

GIN, MORE GIN, BLANC VERMOUTH, STREGA, EAU DE VIE, CHERRY VANILLA BITTERS, PEYCHAUD'S BITTERS, ROSEMARY

YIELD: 1 SERVING
GLASSWARE: MARTINI GLASS

The dance scenes throughout the movie mesmerize the senses, much like this cocktail. The intense red hues, the honeyed flavors of Strega, and the enticing smells of rosemary that all emanate from this low-ABV martini might start to take over and possess you . . .

0.5 ounce London dry gin (Greenhook American Dry Gin recommended)

0.25 ounce Old Tom gin (Greenhook Old Tom Gin recommended)

1.25 ounces Dolin Blanc Vermouth de Chambéry

0.25 ounce Strega

2 barspoons Clear Creek Douglas Fir Brandy

5 dashes Bittercube Cherry Bark Vanilla Bitters

3 dashes Peychaud's Bitters

1 rosemary sprig for garnish

1. Combine all the ingredients, except the garnish, in an ice-filled mixing glass.

2. Stir for 20 to 25 seconds and strain into a chilled martini glass.

3. Garnish with a slapped rosemary sprig.

SALA ROSSA | *SUSPIRIA (1977)*

CAMPARI, SWEET VERMOUTH, WORMWOOD, SODA WATER, APEROL GLASS

YIELD: 1 SERVING
GLASSWARE: HIGHBALL GLASS

A variation on the classic Americano cocktail, named for its popularity among American tourists in Italy. It is inspired by the lead character, Suzy, an American visitor to Freiburg. The Italian roots of the cocktail are a nod to the Italian director and production of the film. Wormwood—long associated with witches—is added, as well as Aperol "broken glass," an element in a riveting scene of the film.

1.5 ounces Campari

1.5 ounces sweet vermouth

3 dashes wormwood tincture, or 1 barspoon absinthe

3 ounces soda water

Aperol Glass for garnish (recipe follows)

1. Combine all the ingredients, except the garnish, in an ice-filled mixing glass.
2. Stir and strain into an ice-filled highball glass.
3. Garnish with Aperol glass.

APEROL GLASS   YIELD: 4 SERVINGS

1. Pour ⅜ inch (1 cm) of Aperol onto a baking sheet.
2. Bake at 200°F for 6 to 12 hours, until it hardens.
3. Remove from the oven and allow to cool, then break into large pieces with a heavy spoon or mallet.

As he does in many of his films, director Dario Argento's own hands are the hands of the killer.

TORN TO PIECES | *SUSPIRIA (2018)*

BEEF TARTARE, BLACK TRUFFLES, CALABRIAN CHILI, CROSTINI, BORAGE FLOWERS

YIELD: 4 SERVINGS
ALLERGIES: DAIRY (OR CHOOSE DAIRY-FREE BREAD), GLUTEN (OR CHOOSE GLUTEN-FREE BREAD)
TOOL: 4-INCH RING MOLD

While this dish may be a little too on the nose for some, we couldn't resist. Much like the film, it is visual, visceral, and with an unmistakable Italian lean.

4 slices white bread

4 tablespoons unsalted butter

1 small black truffle

¼ cup extra virgin olive oil, plus more for serving

1 pound high-quality lean and tender beef, such as sirloin or tenderloin

1½ tablespoons sherry vinegar

1 tablespoon Dijon mustard

¼ cup finely minced shallot

2 tablespoons finely minced capers

2 tablespoons finely minced tender inner celery stalks

2 tablespoons finely minced tender inner celery leaves

2 tablespoons finely minced parsley

2 teaspoons Calabrian chili

2 large egg yolks

1 tablespoon salt

Freshly ground black pepper

Maldon salt (optional)

Borage flowers for garnish

1. Preheat the oven to 200°F.

2. Cut the crust off the bread and slice into bite-size squares or triangles. Transfer to a baking sheet. Melt the butter and brush onto the bread until well saturated. Bake until golden brown and crisp.

3. Shave three to five thin slices from the truffle (reserve the rest) and finely mince. Combine with the olive oil in a small bowl and allow to rest at room temperature for at least 2 hours and up to 24.

4. Clean as much of the fat and connective tissue from the meat as you can. With a very sharp knife, chop the beef into the smallest pieces you can manage.

5. Combine the vinegar, Dijon, shallot, capers, celery stalks and leaves, parsley, chili, egg yolks, salt, and the truffle mixture in a large bowl. Add the beef and stir to integrate thoroughly.

6. To serve, press the beef mixture into a ring mold and turn onto a plate, place a few thin slices of the reserved truffle on top, drizzle with olive oil, season with freshly ground black pepper and a sprinkle of Maldon salt, if using. Garnish each serving with a borage flower. Serve with a few pieces of the toasted bread.

FLESH | *FLESH FOR FRANKENSTEIN (1973)*

GIN, MIDORI, GREEN CHARTREUSE, LIME, EGG WHITE, CHERRY

YIELD: 1 SERVING
GLASSWARE: COUPE GLASS

Unlike the classic Universal take on Frankenstein's monster, *Flesh for Frankenstein*'s creations are not depicted with green skin. We made a bright green drink anyway because we like Chartreuse and Midori. They make a very strange pairing but not as strange as this film.

0.75 ounce gin
0.75 ounce Midori
0.75 ounce Green Chartreuse
0.75 ounce fresh lime juice
0.5 ounce simple syrup
1 egg white
Amarena cherry for garnish

1. Combine all the ingredients in a cocktail shaking tin and shake vigorously without ice. Add ice and shake again.

2. Strain through a fine-mesh strainer into a chilled coupe glass.

3. Garnish with an Amarena cherry.

Special effects were early work from Carlo Rambaldi, who would later go on to do the special effects for *E.T.* (1982). The original idea came from director Roman Polanski, who had met writer-director Paul Morrissey when promoting his film *What?*, with Morrissey stating that Polanski felt he would be "a natural person to make a 3-D film about Frankenstein."

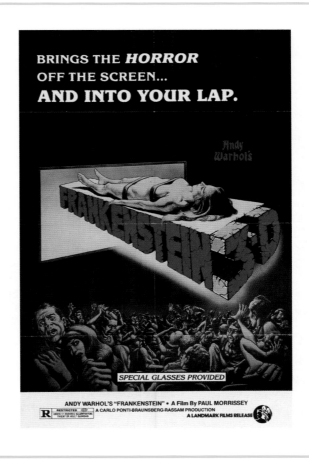

ASH VS. EVIL ASH |

ARMY OF DARKNESS (1992)

SHORT RIB, HANGER STEAK, POMME PUREE, CARROT PUREE

YIELD: 4 SERVINGS
ALLERGY: DAIRY
TOOLS: MORTAR AND PESTLE, RICER

Two dishes in one that seem the same on the surface but are different in their core. Just as Ash does battle with Evil Ash, these two beef dishes will battle it out on your plate.

FOR THE SHORT RIBS

2 tablespoons extra
  virgin olive oil

Salt and freshly ground
  black pepper

4 (12- to 16-ounce) pieces
  bone-in short rib

5 garlic cloves

1 red onion, coarsely chopped

4 celery stalks

2 large carrots, rough chopped

4 tablespoons tomato paste

2 cups red wine

1 ounce fresh thyme

1 ounce fresh sage

1 cup demi-glace

FOR THE HANGER STEAK

4 garlic cloves

1 tablespoon sugar

1 teaspoon salt

1 teaspoon freshly
  ground black pepper

1 teaspoon chili powder

Four 8-ounce pieces
  hanger steak

FOR THE POMME PUREE

8 cups water

¼ cup salt

4 Yukon Gold or other
  waxy potatoes

1 cup heavy cream

2 garlic cloves

½ pound (2 sticks)
  unsalted butter

FOR THE CARROT PUREE

5 large carrots, peeled
  and thinly sliced

⅓ cup + 4 teaspoons water

7 tablespoons unsalted butter

⅓ teaspoon salt

Freshly ground black pepper

1 teaspoon fresh lemon juice

TO MAKE THE SHORT RIBS

1. Preheat the oven to 250°F.

2. Heat the oil in a Dutch oven until almost smoking.

3. Salt and pepper the short ribs generously.

4. Place each short rib, top down, into the pot and sear until browned.

5. Remove the ribs and set aside.

6. Lower the heat to medium-low and add the garlic, red onion, celery, and carrots. Cook until the carrots brown.

7. Add the tomato paste, deglaze the pot with wine, then return the beef to the pot.

8. Tie the thyme and sage together and add to the pot with demi-glace.

9. Cover the pot and cook in the oven for 4 hours, or until tender and the bone comes loose.

CONTINUED ▶

10. Remove the beef, strain the pan juices, and return them to the pot. Over medium heat, reduce the juices until your desired thickness.

TO MAKE THE HANGER STEAK

1. Line a baking sheet with aluminum foil. Turn the oven to BROIL.

2. Combine the garlic, sugar, salt, pepper, and chili powder in a mortar and grind together with a pestle.

3. Rub each steak thoroughly with spice rub.

4. Lay the steak on the prepared pan and place in the oven.

5. Broil on each side for 3 minutes, or until starting to scorch on each side.

6. Remove from the oven and let the steak rest for 5 to 8 minutes before cutting.

TO MAKE THE POMME PUREE

1. Combine the water, salt, and potatoes in a large pot, bring to a boil, and cook the potatoes until soft.

2. Pour off the water and allow the potatoes to cool.

3. When cool to the touch, peel the potatoes and run them through a ricer into a bowl.

4. Combine the cream and garlic in a small pot and heat until the garlic becomes tender. Discard the garlic.

5. Mix the garlic-infused cream into the potatoes until combined.

6. Whisk in the butter, 1 tablespoon at a time.

TO MAKE THE CARROT PUREE

1. Bring the carrots and water to a boil in a pot and then lower the heat to a simmer.

2. Cook until most of the water is absorbed and the carrots are tender.

3. Place the carrots in a blender and blend on low speed while adding the butter, 1 tablespoon at a time.

4. Add the salt, the pepper to taste, and the lemon juice.

TO ASSEMBLE

1. Place a large spoonful of potato puree on each plate, then drag the spoon through it in a curved manner.

2. At the end of the curve, place an equal amount of carrot puree, then drag a spoon through it in the opposite direction, ending at the potato.

3. Slice the steak into five to seven pieces, then arrange along the carrot puree.

4. Place the short ribs on top of the potato puree and top with the desired amount of pan sauce.

Director William Lustig (*Maniac*, *Vigilante*) makes a cameo as a supermarket customer credited as "Fake Shemp."

BRUNCH MOVIES:

SHAKE OFF A LONG NIGHT WITH THESE COMFORT FILMS

A more chill and relaxed cousin to the Midnite Movie, you're invited to meet old and new friends in the form of comfort food and movies. Be it an exciting adventure, cozy romance, something from your teenage years you enjoy revisiting, or a first-time viewing experience, there's nothing like easing into a lazy day with good food and a movie to start.

YOU'VE BEEN TRYING TO MAKE US TRY THIS TOFU | *BUT I'M A CHEERLEADER* (1999)

SOY AND MAPLE–MARINATED TOFU, LETTUCE, TOMATO, VEGAN MAYO

YIELD: 1 SERVING
ALLERGIES: GLUTEN, SOY

The TLT: A classic midwestern sandwich made vegan. During the intervention scene, Megan's switch to vegetarianism is a sure sign to her family that she is a lesbian. A slice of tofu is held up as evidence.

FOR THE MARINATED TOFU

1 pound extra-firm tofu

1 cup soy sauce

⅓ cup pure maple syrup

½ cup water

1 teaspoon liquid smoke

1 cup white rice flour

1 cup oil

FOR THE VEGAN MAYO

1 cup aquafava (reserved juice from can of chickpeas)

½ teaspoon salt

1½ teaspoons fresh lemon juice

½ teaspoon sugar

1 cup oil

FOR ASSEMBLY (PER SANDWICH)

2 slices bread, toasted

2 pieces butter lettuce

2 slices tomato, salted

> Tofu is believed to have been invented in China around 2,000 years ago. The legend is that a cook was experimenting with adding nigari to flavor soybeans and ended up making curd. Nigari is still often used in modern tofu production.

TO MAKE THE MARINATED TOFU

1. Press the tofu between two plates and apply a weight to the top. Let the tofu sit for an hour, trying to get out as much liquid as possible.

2. Mix together the soy sauce, maple syrup, water, and liquid smoke in a large bowl.

3. Slice the drained tofu horizontally into four pieces and submerge in the liquid.

4. Cover and let marinate in the refrigerator for 24 hours or more.

5. Remove the tofu from the liquid and place on paper towels to dry.

6. When as dry as possible, coat each piece of tofu with rice flour, completely covering it.

7. Heat the oil in a deep skillet until just about smoking.

8. Fry each piece of tofu until crispy.

TO MAKE THE VEGAN MAYO

1. Mix together the aquafava, salt, lemon juice, and sugar in a glass.

2. While using an immersion blender in the mixture, slowly add the oil.

3. Blend until thickened.

TO ASSEMBLE

1. Spread the vegan mayonnaise on each slice of bread.

2. Stack the lettuce, tomato, and tofu.

CONTINUED ▷

Director Jamie Babbit took inspiration for the "reparative therapy" shown at the True Directions camp in *But I'm a Cheerleader* from her mother's occupation, which was running an in-patient treatment program for teenagers with drug and alcohol problems called New Directions.

PREPARE TO GET BASHED!

BOOKSMART (2019)

EMPANADA PUFFS, MEATY MARINARA SAUCE, OPTIONAL CBD OIL

YIELD: 4 SERVINGS
ALLERGIES: DAIRY, GLUTEN
TOOL: FOOD PROCESSOR
(OPTIONAL)

These small "empanada" puffs are based on the pizzas ordered in one of the movie's key scenes. CBD oil is a play on "getting high," as the characters in the movie do. We named it after Jared's motivational remark to the girls before entering the party on his yacht.

Note on CBD: After first checking what your local regulations say, always consider the potency of the product you're using before adding it to your food. The potency of a teaspoon of low-strength (10 mg/ml) oil will be very different from a teaspoon of a high-potency oil (33.3 mg/ml), and CBD affects people differently.

FOR THE FILLING

- 1½ cups canned tomato
- 2 teaspoons canola oil
- 11 ounces hot Italian sausage
- 3 garlic cloves, peeled and minced
- ⅜ cup peeled and small-diced carrot
- ⅜ cup small-diced onion
- Rounded tablespoon tomato paste
- 2 tablespoons white wine
- 1 tablespoon dried oregano
- 1 teaspoon dried basil
- 1½ tablespoons dried parsley
- 1 teaspoon sugar
- 3 tablespoons vegetable stock
- ¾ teaspoon Worcestershire sauce
- Scant teaspoon crushed red pepper flakes
- ⅔ teaspoon dried thyme
- 1⅔ teaspoons balsamic vinegar
- 4 ounces shredded mozzarella
- 1 to 2 teaspoons CBD oil (optional; see note)

TO MAKE THE FILLING

1. Puree the canned tomato in a blender or food processor and set aside.

2. In a large skillet, add 1 teaspoon of the oil. Remove the sausage from its casing and add to the skillet. Once cooked through, remove the meat from the skillet, drain, and set aside. Discard the rendered fat.

3. Heat the remaining 1 teaspoon of oil in the same skillet, and sweat the garlic, carrot, and onion until translucent.

4. Add the tomato paste, stirring occasionally. Cook until the tomato paste begins to brown.

5. Deglaze the pan with the white wine and reduce until the liquid is almost evaporated.

6. Add the pureed canned tomato, cooked sausage meat, and all the remaining ingredients, except the CBD oil, and cook until the filling reaches your desired consistency.

7. Let cool completely, then add the CBD oil, mixing well.

CONTINUED ▷

There was a brief moment in NYC when CBD was allowed to be added to all kinds of food and drink items—in your coffee, cocktails, and food. Ultimately it was deemed too unregulated and disallowed, but we have a sneaking suspicion CBD and THC will be legalized at some point soon in New York.

FOR THE EMPANADAS

**Eight 6-inch empanada
dough sheets**

2 tablespoons water

1 quart canola oil for frying

TO MAKE THE EMPANADAS

1. Split the empanada dough sheets in half.

2. Place 2 to 3 tablespoons of the filling in the center of the split dough.

3. Dip a fingertip into the water. Run along the edge of dough.

4. Seal by pressing down with a fork along the edges, creating a crimped look. The empanadas can be frozen at this point for later use.

5. Heat the oil to 350°F in a large pot. Place three to five puffs into the oil at a time and cook for 4 to 6 minutes (6 to 8, if frozen). Remove from the oil with a metal strainer and place on a paper towel to drain.

This was Olivia Wilde's directorial debut. Beanie Feldstein read the script for another role that finally was ultimately excluded. When Olivia Wilde saw her, she decided to give her the costar role of Molly.

WILDE & FREE | *BOOKSMART (2019)*

RUM, PISCO, LIME, AMONTILLADO SHERRY, PASSION FRUIT, GRAPEFRUIT, ORANGE, TIKI BITTERS, SPARKLING WINE

YIELD: 1 SERVING
GLASSWARE: COLLINS GLASS

Drinks at grad parties can be a total bust, and it's always better to BYOB. You'll be prepared for anything with this cocktail, but remember . . . *beware the golden starfish!!!*

Pro Tip: Add the sparkling wine *before* you add your ice in your collins glass to better incorporate the drink.

1.25 ounces white rum

0.5 ounce pisco

0.5 ounce fresh lime juice

0.5 ounce Amontillado sherry (Lustau Amontillado Los Arcos preferred)

0.75 ounce Half Slytherin–Half Ravenclaw Liqueur (recipe follows)

2 dashes Bittermens 'Elemakule Tiki Bitters

Sparkling wine to top (Prosecco or Cava recommended; see Pro Tip)

Lime wheel for garnish

1. Combine all the ingredients, except the sparkling wine and garnish, in an ice-filled mixing tin.

2. Shake vigorously for 5 to 10 seconds and double strain into a collins glass. Top with the sparkling wine.

3. Garnish with a lime wheel and serve immediately.

HALF SLYTHERIN–HALF RAVENCLAW LIQUEUR **YIELD:** 15 TO 18 SERVINGS

1 cup passion fruit liqueur (Alize preferred)

1 cup grapefruit juice

1 cup fresh orange juice

1⅓ cups sugar

1. Combine all the ingredients in a nonreactive pot and bring to a boil.

2. Lower the temperature to medium-low and simmer for 10 minutes.

3. Remove from the heat and allow to cool, then bottle and refrigerate.

> We totally made up Half Slytherin–Half Ravenclaw liqueur based on a quote from the movie. But we were very pleased with how it turned out.

PARIS STILTON CLUB | *THE BLING RING* (2013)

ROASTED TURKEY BREAST, BACON, LETTUCE, HEIRLOOM TOMATO, STILTON AIOLI, POTATO CHIPS

YIELD: 1 SERVING
ALLERGIES: DAIRY, GLUTEN, POSSIBLY SOY (OR CHOOSE SOY-FREE MAYO)
TOOL: FRILLY TOOTHPICKS

This is a regular club sandwich that has been elevated above its standing with herbes de Provence and a fancy aioli. In the movie, the Bling Ring gang see Paris Hilton at a club and then rob her house several times, attaining her status for a brief moment via her expensive property.

FOR THE TURKEY BREAST

1 tablespoon extra virgin olive oil

1 tablespoon herbes de Provence

2 tablespoons unsalted butter

2 garlic cloves, minced

1 teaspoon salt

½ teaspoon freshly ground black pepper

1 turkey breast, skin on

FOR THE STILTON AIOLI

2 garlic cloves, minced

2 teaspoons horseradish

1 cup mayonnaise

6 ounces Stilton, crumbled

½ teaspoon freshly ground black pepper

FOR ASSEMBLY

3 slices white bread, toasted

2 pieces butter lettuce

2 slices heirloom tomato

4 slices bacon, cooked crispy and cooled

Potato chips for serving

TO MAKE THE TURKEY BREAST

1. Preheat the oven to 400°F.

2. Grease the bottom of a baking pan with the olive oil.

3. Mix the herbes de Provence, butter, garlic, salt, and pepper together in a small bowl.

4. Peel back the skin of the turkey and rub in the herbed butter, then put the skin back in place.

5. Place the turkey in the prepared pan and roast for about an hour, or until the internal temperature reaches 165°F.

6. Remove from the oven and allow to cool completely before slicing.

TO MAKE THE STILTON AIOLI

Stir all the aioli ingredients together in a small bowl.

TO ASSEMBLE

1. Apply the aioli to one side of each slice of bread.

2. Layer a slice of bread with a piece of lettuce, a tomato slice, 2 slices of bacon, and 2 slices of turkey. Place another slice of bread on top and repeat.

3. Top with the third slice of bread and put a frilly toothpick in each corner.

4. Slice the sandwich into quarters.

5. Serve with potato chips.

CONTINUED ▶

Penicillium roqueforti is the bacteria used to make Stilton. It is the same one used to make Roquefort, Danish blue, Cabrales, Gorgonzola, and other blue cheeses.

Kirsten Dunst, having previously worked with director Sofia Coppola on *The Virgin Suicides* (1999) and *Marie Antoinette* (2006), makes a cameo in the film as herself. This scene was not part of the original script and was incorporated into the film after Dunst visited the set.

SACRAMENT OF THE BODY

LADY BIRD (2017)

GRAPE BRUSCHETTA, GOAT CHEESE, "NONCONSECRATED" WAFER, BALSAMIC REDUCTION

YIELD: 12 SERVINGS
ALLERGIES: DAIRY, GLUTEN

The movie starts with Lady Bird and her mother listening to *The Grapes of Wrath* on tape. The movie is set in California and Humboldt Fog is a Californian goat milk cheese with a layer of edible ash. The Ash Wednesday scene shows the family with ash crosses on their forehead. Lady Bird is seen eating communion wafers like snacks, saying it's okay because they're "not consecrated."

FOR THE GRAPE BRUCHETTA

1 tablespoon red wine

1 tablespoon extra
  virgin olive oil

1 tablespoon honey

1 teaspoon salt

½ teaspoon freshly
  ground black pepper

1 pound grapes, small diced

2 tablespoons thinly
  sliced scallion

⅛ cup finely diced red onion

**FOR THE BALSAMIC
REDUCTION**

2 cups balsamic vinegar

FOR ASSEMBLY

12 round crackers

6 ounces Humboldt Fog
Soft-Ripened Goat Milk Cheese

Humboldt Fog is a goat milk cheese made by Cypress Grove of Arcata, California, in Humboldt County. It is named for the local ocean fog that rolls in from Humboldt Bay.

TO MAKE THE GRAPE BRUSCHETTA

1. Mix together the wine, olive oil, honey, salt, and pepper in a small bowl.

2. Mix together the grapes, scallion, and red onion in a separate bowl.

3. Pour the wine mixture on top of the grape mixture and mix thoroughly.

TO MAKE THE BALSAMIC REDUCTION

1. Bring the balsamic vinegar to a boil in a small, nonreactive, heavy-bottomed saucepan.

2. Lower the heat to a simmer and, while skimming with a rubber spatula, continue to cook until reduced to ½ cup, about 20 minutes

3. Remove from the heat and allow to cool.

TO ASSEMBLE

1. Layer a heaping tablespoon of grape bruschetta onto each cracker.

2. Top each with a 0.5-ounce slice of Humboldt Fog.

3. Top with balsamic reduction.

CONTINUED ▷

In addition to this being Greta Gerwig's solo feature directorial debut, her on-set daily consumption of Diet Coke and Cheetos led the crew to name this food and drink combo "The Greta."

SACRAMENT OF THE BLOOD

LADY BIRD (2017)

CALIFORNIA-STYLE RED SANGRIA

YIELD: 8 TO 10 SERVINGS
GLASSWARE: LARGE WINE GLASSES

A classic sangria with the addition of prickly pear soda. This recipe plays on the same sacramental theme as the food special, as the film takes place in Sacramento, adding yet another layer.

One 750-milliliter bottle full-bodied California red wine

3 ounces triple sec

3 ounces brandy

6 ounces fresh blood orange juice

2 ounces Ginger Syrup (recipe follows)

0.25 ounce Angostura Bitters

12 ounces prickly pear soda

Blood orange wheels for garnish

1. Mix together all the ingredients, except the garnish, in a 2-liter pitcher.
2. Pour large ice-filled wine glasses.
3. Garnish with blood orange wheels.

GINGER SYRUP YIELD: 1½ CUPS

1½ cups water

1¾ cups sugar

6 ounces fresh ginger

1. Combine all the ingredients in a blender and blend.
2. Transfer to a saucepan and simmer over low heat for 30 minutes.
3. Remove from the heat, strain, and allow to cool completely.

> Prickly pear is also known as tuna fruit. This pinkish red fruit tastes a bit like watermelon and adds a nice flavor to the sangria.

FEED UP TIME

BEASTS OF THE SOUTHERN WILD (2012)

HUSH PUPPY–BATTERED CATFISH, TABASCO HONEY BUTTER

YIELD: 4 SERVINGS
ALLERGIES: DAIRY, EGG, FISH, GLUTEN

In this film set in southern Louisiana, Hushpuppy, played by the talented newcomer Quvenzhané Wallis, catches a catfish with her bare hands and prepares it with her father, Wink.

FOR THE TABASCO HONEY BUTTER

½ **pound (2 sticks) unsalted butter, at room temperature**

1 **cup honey**

¼ **cup Tabasco**

1 **tablespoon kosher salt**

FOR THE CATFISH

1 **cup yellow cornmeal**

¼ **cup all-purpose flour, plus more for dredging**

1½ **teaspoons baking powder**

1 **tablespoon kosher salt**

2 **ounces canned pimiento or roasted red pepper, drained and small diced**

1 **scallion, sliced thinly**

1 **large egg**

1½ **cups buttermilk**

Canola oil for deep frying

1½ **pounds catfish fillets, cut into four 6-ounce portions**

Cajun seasoning

TO MAKE THE TABASCO HONEY BUTTER

Using a stand mixer fitted with the paddle attachment, or a medium bowl and a hand mixer, beat the butter with honey, Tabasco, and salt until fully incorporated and slightly fluffy.

TO MAKE THE CATFISH

1. Combine the cornmeal, flour, baking powder, salt, pimiento, and scallion in a large bowl and mix well. If you treat the additions to a batter like this one like a dry ingredient, they will remain mixed within the batter and not sink to the bottom.

2. Whisk in the egg and buttermilk, making sure not to overmix.

3. Heat the oil to 350°F in a tall-sided 4-quart or larger saucepan.

4. Pat dry the catfish fillets and dredge in the flour mixture. Once dredged, dip into the batter and fry in the oil until golden brown.

5. Remove from the oil and season with Cajun seasoning.

6. Serve with the Tabasco honey butter.

CONTINUED ▶

> Hush puppies often attributed to hunters, fishermen, or other cooks who would fry some basic cornmeal mixture (possibly that they had been bread-coating or battering their own food with) and feed it to their dogs to "hush the puppies" during cookouts or fish fries.

According to director Benh Zeitlin, Louisiana Bayou native Quvenzhané Wallis (Nazie, as she is called) beat out almost 4,000 other area kids considered for the lead role.

VEGETARIAN KATZ

WHEN HARRY MET SALLY (1989)

CELERY ROOT "PASTRAMI," CASHEW THOUSAND ISLAND, SAUERKRAUT, GRUYÈRE, SPELT RYE

YIELD: 4 SERVINGS
ALLERGIES: DAIRY, GLUTEN, SOY, TREE NUTS (CASHEW)
TOOL: SLICER

From one of the most famous scenes in movie history, Harry and Sally are having sandwiches at Katz's Deli while they discuss pleasure. We put a Nitehawk twist on it, making this classic sandwich vegetarian with a deliciously cured celery root "pastrami." It's so good that everyone will be asking for what she's having.

Note: You can make this a Vegan Katz by subbing out the Gruyère with your favorite vegan cheese slices.

FOR THE CELERY ROOT "PASTRAMI"

3 quarts water

2 cups kosher salt

1 cup granulated sugar

½ cup dark brown sugar

1 tablespoon coriander seeds

4 garlic cloves, crushed

2 tablespoons liquid smoke

½ cup red wine vinegar

2 cups ketchup

4 celery roots, peeled

FOR THE RUB

6 tablespoons ground coriander

3 tablespoons yellow mustard seeds

5 teaspoons dark brown sugar

5 tablespoons smoked paprika

2 teaspoons garlic powder

1 tablespoon ground cloves

2 tablespoons + 1 teaspoon freshly ground black pepper

5 teaspoons salt

FOR THE CASHEW THOUSAND ISLAND

3¾ cups raw cashews

7 tablespoons fresh lemon juice

⅓ cup apple cider vinegar

⅓ cup pickle chip brine

⅓ cup ketchup

Rounded ½ teaspoon salt

1 teaspoon mustard seeds

2 teaspoons garlic powder

2 teaspoons soy sauce

3 tablespoons agave syrup

1 pint pickle chips, diced

FOR ASSEMBLY

Rye bread

Sauerkraut

Sliced Gruyère

Pickles

TO MAKE THE BRINE

1. Bring all the brine ingredients, except the celery roots, to a boil in a saucepan.

2. Place the celery roots in a heatproof bowl and pour the brine over them.

3. Let sit for 1 day, or more if possible, in the refrigerator.

TO MAKE THE RUB

1. Mix all the spices together.

2. Roll the celery roots in the spice mixture and set on a drying rack.

3. When dry and ready to serve, slice the celery roots as thinly as possible.

CONTINUED ▶

TO MAKE THE CASHEW THOUSAND ISLAND

1. The night before, place the cashews in a bowl, cover with water, and set aside.
2. Drain the cashews.
3. Place all the dressing ingredients in a blender and blend until smooth.

TO ASSEMBLE

1. Toast two pieces of rye bread for each sandwich.
2. Coat each slice of bread with the cashew Thousand Island.
3. Place a skillet over medium heat. Loosely layer in the sliced celery root "pastrami," place a pinch of sauerkraut on top, and add Gruyère to cover.
4. Add a tablespoon of water and cover the skillet until the cheese is melted and the celery root "pastrami" is hot.
5. Place the melted cheesy stack on the toasted bread. Slice in half.
6. Serve with a pickle.

In the famous faked orgasm scene at Katz's Deli, the woman who delivers the line "I'll have what she's having" is director Rob Reiner's mother, Estelle Reiner.

ANOTHER QUESO? | *BOYHOOD (2014)*

LIQUID GOLD QUESO, PICKLED JALAPEÑO, TORTILLA CHIPS

YIELD: 2 SERVINGS
ALLERGY: DAIRY
TOOL: SLOW COOKER
(OPTIONAL)

In this coming-of-age story set in Texas, spanning 15 years, the protagonist and his girlfriend find themselves at an Austin diner in the wee hours of the morning. When asked what they were doing there, they exclaim, "Queso!" A staple of any good Texan's late-night diet!

FOR THE PICKLED JALAPEÑO

1 pound jalapeño peppers, sliced ¼ inch thick

¼ cup sliced Spanish or white onion

¼ cup peeled and sliced carrot

2 cups apple cider vinegar

2 cups water

2 teaspoons coriander seeds

¼ cup granulated sugar

FOR THE QUESO

2 cups milk

½ cup sour cream

½ cup canned peeled, diced tomatoes

1 canned chipotle pepper

2 pounds Velveeta

1 pound jalapeño Velveeta

Tortilla chips

TO MAKE THE PICKLED JALAPEÑO

1. Pack the sliced jalapeños tightly into a heatproof glass and top with the sliced onion and carrot.

2. Bring the vinegar, water, coriander seeds, and sugar to a boil in a nonreactive saucepan.

3. Very carefully pour the brine over the sliced jalapeños and vegetables.

4. Let cool to room temperature. Then top with a lid to make as airtight as possible and chill completely in the fridge. Will stay good for 1 to 2 months, refrigerated.

TO MAKE THE QUESO

1. Combine the milk, sour cream, tomatoes, chipotle pepper, and ½ cup of pickled jalapeño in a blender or blend using an immersion blender.

2. Dice the two Velveetas and put into 2-quart saucepot or slow cooker along with the pureed vegetables mixture.

3. If using a pot, place over low heat and stir often to keep from scorching until the cheeses are completely melted.

4. If using a slow cooker, place all the ingredients in the machine and set to MEDIUM-LOW to melt the cheeses.

5. Whisk to combine and serve with tortilla chips.

CONTINUED ▷

The film took 12 years to make, with each scene being filmed in one-week increments.

IT'S SO ABSURD I HAVE TO BE HERE ON SATURDAY | *THE BREAKFAST CLUB (1985)*

GOAT CHEESE, SMOKED SALMON, CHIVE WHIPPED CREAM, DUCK FAT AND RED WINE HOLLANDAISE, EVERYTHING BAGEL CHIP

YIELD: 4 SERVINGS
ALLERGIES: DAIRY, EGG, FISH, GLUTEN

While Claire may have helped introduce sushi to the US mainstream, this re-creation uses some traditional brunch ingredients that would be a welcome addition to any brunch spread.

FOR THE HOLLANDAISE

1 cup red wine

½ shallot, minced

½ teaspoon whole black peppercorns

2 thyme sprigs

2 large egg yolks

1 teaspoon red wine vinegar

2 cups duck fat, melted but not hot

Salt and freshly ground black pepper

FOR THE WHIPPED CREAM

2 tablespoons chopped fresh chives

1 teaspoon water

1 cup heavy cream

Salt

FOR SERVING

8 ounces sliced smoked salmon

8 ounces Westfield Farm Capri Goat Cheese

Everything bagel chips or toasted everything bagel

TO MAKE THE HOLLANDAISE

1. Combine the red wine, shallot, peppercorns, and thyme in a small saucepot. Over medium heat, reduce by two-thirds. Strain through a fine-mesh strainer and set aside.

2. In a heatproof, nonreactive bowl set over a pot of water at just under a simmer, combine the egg yolks and red wine vinegar. Whip until frothy and light. You want to be able draw a figure eight into the yolks. Slowly start to incorporate the duck fat into the whipped yolks. Season with salt and pepper.

TO MAKE THE WHIPPED CREAM

1. In a blender, combine the chives with the water until smooth.

2. With a mixer or by hand, whip the cream to soft peaks in a large bowl, fold in the blended chives, and season with salt to taste

TO SERVE

1. To mimic pieces of sushi, lay the smoked salmon in a single layer, spread the cheese across the salmon, and very gently roll into a log. Slice into rounds.

2. Place the rolled salmon on a plate, cut side up, with the chive whipped cream and hollandaise on the side to mimic wasabi and soy sauce Serve with everything bagel chips or a toasted everything bagel.

> Claire's sushi lunch was meant to show how different she was from the rest of the group but it also served as one of America's first introductions to sushi in pop culture.

The anthemic beginning and end credits song, "Don't You Forget About Me," performed by Simple Minds, was originally offered to Bryan Ferry, then Billy Idol, who both turned it down.

The "chilled monkey brains" in the movie were made from custard and raspberry sauce.

EYEBALL SOUP

INDIANA JONES AND THE TEMPLE OF DOOM (1984)

RUM, BITTERS, ORGEAT, LEMON

YIELD: 1 SERVING
ALLERGY: TREE NUTS (ALMOND)
GLASSWARE: SMALL METAL BOWL
GARNISH: PLASTIC EYEBALLS

This Angostura Bitters–based cocktail mimics the murky reddish brown of the eyeball soup in the film. We make it with Old Monk Rum, a nod to the Indian shaman in the film.

1 ounce Old Monk Rum
1 ounce Angostura Bitters
1 ounce orgeat syrup
0.75 ounce fresh lemon juice

1. Combine all the ingredients in an ice-filled cocktail shaking tin.
2. Shake and strain into a small, chilled metal bowl.
3. Garnish with plastic eyeballs.

TRUFFLE SHUFFLE POPCORN

THE GOONIES (1985)

POPCORN, TRUFFLE BUTTER, CITRIC SALT

YIELD: 1 SERVING
ALLERGY: DAIRY

You'll be dancing like Chunk when you taste our iconic Nitehawk popcorn. There was a mini revolt when we removed this seasonal popcorn from our menu, so we brought it back permanently as the namesake.

3 tablespoons clarified butter
1 teaspoon truffle oil
⅛ teaspoon salt
⅛ teaspoon citric acid
2 quarts popped popcorn

1. Mix together the butter and truffle oil in a small bowl.
2. Mix together the salt and citric acid in a separate small bowl.
3. Place the popcorn in a large metal bowl and top with the butter and salt mixtures.
4. Cover with another large bowl and shake until completely mixed.

Cyndi Lauper cowrote the theme song, "The Goonies 'R' Good Enough," and shot a 12-minute music video that features a cameo by Steven Spielberg. Lauper plays Cyndi (a new Goonie recruit), The Bangles play pirates, and André the Giant plays Sloth.

Dogs known as "truffle hounds" are used for finding truffles, rather than pigs, since pigs have been known to eat the truffles themselves. However, many truffle traditionalists will argue that pig noses are more sensitive.

GOONIES NEVER SAY DIE (HEY, YOU GUYS!!!) | *THE GOONIES* (1985)

PEANUT-INFUSED RYE WHISKEY, AMARO MONTENEGRO, CRÈME DE CACAO, POBLANO CHILE

YIELD: 1 SERVING
ALLERGIES: GLUTEN, PEANUTS
GLASSWARE: COUPE OR MARTINI GLASS

Sometimes you just want to be a "Sloth" on the couch, turn on the TV, and rip into a Baby Ruth. Though with this Manhattan recipe, make sure it doesn't fall on the floor—the cleanup might make you angry.

2 ounces Peanut-Infused High West (recipe follows)

1 ounce Amaro Montenegro

0.25 ounce Giffard Crème de Cacao Blanc

0.1 ounce Ancho Reyes Verde Chile Poblano Liqueur

1 dropperful (about 1 ml) Cruzan Blackstrap Rum

Mini Baby Ruth candy for garnish

1. Build all the ingredients, garnish, in an ice-filled mixing glass.
2. Stir for 10 to 15 seconds and strain into a couple or martini glass.
3. Garnish with a mini Baby Ruth candy.

PEANUT-INFUSED HIGH WEST YIELD: 10 TO 12 SERVINGS

One 750-milliliter bottle High West Rendezvous Rye

½ cup Planter's Honey Roasted Peanuts, crushed

1. Combine all the ingredients in a quart-size container and let infuse for at least 12 hours.
2. Strain through a fine strainer set into a funnel, back into the bottle.

I GOT YOU BABE | *GROUNDHOG DAY (1993)*

GIN, COCCHI AMERICANO, COINTREAU, LEMON, ORANGE MARMALADE

YIELD: 1 SERVING
GLASSWARE: COUPE OR MARTINI GLASS

This song wakes Phil during his Groundhog Day time loop, a terrible reminder that he is still caught in this particular brand of hell. This is a cocktail I could see Phil ordering for breakfast—if nothing really matters, why not start early and make yourself a strong breakfast cocktail?

0.75 ounce gin
0.75 ounce Cocchi Americano
0.75 ounce Cointreau
0.75 ounce fresh lemon juice
1 heavy barspoon
  orange marmalade
Lemon peel for garnish

1. Combine all ingredients, except the garnish, in a cocktail shaker. Stir without ice for a minute or so to incorporate the jam into the cocktail.
2. Add ice to the shaker and shake vigorously until very cold. Fine strain into a chilled stemmed glass.
3. Garnish with a thin lemon peel.

I AM "A" GOD | *GROUNDHOG DAY (1993)*

EGG-IN-A-BASKET BREAKFAST SANDWICH WITH BACON, SAUSAGE, AMERICAN CHEESE, MAPLE SYRUP

YIELD: 1 SERVING
ALLERGIES: DAIRY, EGG, GLUTEN

Phil has decided he is immortal and has given up on trying to eat healthy. This is a calorie-laden breakfast sandwich fit for the gods.

3 strips bacon
2 breakfast sausages
3 large eggs
¼ cup heavy cream
1 tablespoon unsalted butter
2 thick slices bread,
  such as Texas Toast
2 slices American cheese
2 tablespoons pure
  maple syrup

1. Heat a large skillet and cook the bacon and sausage all the way through. Remove from the skillet, slice the sausage in half, and set the bacon and sausage aside.
2. Combine the cream with 1 of the eggs. Scramble the egg in a small skillet and set aside.
3. To the large skillet, add the butter over medium heat.
4. Cut a hole in the center of both pieces of bread and place the bread slices in the large skillet.
5. Crack 1 egg into each hole and cook until done on the underside, then flip.
6. Place 1 slice of the cheese on each piece of egg-filled toast. Cover the pan and cook until the cheese is melted and the eggs are to your desired doneness.
7. Assemble the sandwich by placing one of the pieces of toast, cheese side up, on a plate. Top with the bacon, sausage, scrambled egg, and the second piece of toast, cheese side down.
8. Finish by pouring maple syrup over the top.

THE DUDE ABIDES | *THE BIG LEBOWSKI* (1998)

STOUT, COFFEE-INFUSED VODKA, ANCHO CHILE, WALNUT, SALTED HONEY SYRUP, EGG WHITE

YIELD: 1 SERVING
ALLERGIES: EGG, TREE NUTS (WALNUT)
GLASSWARE: ROCKS GLASS

Jackie Treehorn mixes a hell of a Caucasian. So do we.

3 ounces nitro stout

1 ounce coffee-infused vodka

0.5 ounce ancho chile liqueur

0.25 ounce walnut liqueur

0.25 ounce Salted Honey Syrup (recipe follows)

1 egg white

1. Place a large, square ice cube in a rocks glass and pour the nitro stout to the top of the cube.

2. Combine the remaining ingredients in a cocktail shaking tin, adding the egg white last. Shake vigorously without ice. Add ice and shake again.

3. Strain through a fine-mesh strainer into the stout-filled rocks glass.

SALTED HONEY SYRUP YIELD: 1 CUP

1 cup honey

1 cup water

1 tablespoon kosher salt

1. Combine the ingredients in a saucepan and bring to a soft boil.

2. Remove from the heat and allow to cool completely.

Before filming a scene, Jeff Bridges would frequently ask the Coen brothers, "Did The Dude burn one on the way over?" If they said he had, he would rub his knuckles in his eyes before doing a take to make his eyes appear bloodshot.

CARRIED A WATERMELON |

DIRTY DANCING (1987)

TEQUILA, MEZCAL, APEROL, WATERMELON SYRUP, LIME, ALLSPICE, MINERAL WATER

YIELD: 1 SERVING
GLASSWARE: PILSNER GLASS

Dancing with a professional can be very intimidating—it helps to have a drink to loosen up. And if you're going to carry a watermelon, make sure to enjoy this agave-based watermelon "cooler" while watching this '80s classic.

1 ounce Espolòn Reposado Tequila

0.33 ounce mezcal

0.25 ounce Aperol

1.33 ounces Watermelon Syrup (recipe follows)

0.66 ounce fresh lime juice

2 barspoons agave syrup

1 dash St. Elizabeth Allspice Dram

Very effervescent mineral water (Topo Chico preferred) to top

Watermelon wedge for garnish

1. Combine all the ingredients, except the mineral water and garnish, in a mixing tin.

2. Shake to combine and strain into an ice-filled pilsner glass. Top with mineral water.

3. Garnish with a watermelon wedge.

WATERMELON SYRUP   YIELD: 18 TO 22 SERVINGS

One 12-ounce can Montauk Session Ale Beer

1 pound sugar

2 cups fresh watermelon juice

1. Combine the beer and sugar in a saucepan and bring to a boil.

2. Add the watermelon juice and any pulp to the pot and keep over high heat until all the ingredients are incorporated, less than 5 minutes.

3. Remove from the heat and strain when cooled. Refrigerate.

CONTINUED ▷

Because he had clashed with her while filming *Red Dawn* (1984), Patrick Swayze had to convince Jennifer Grey to make *Dirty Dancing*, as she still disliked him.

SAUCE ON THE SIDE | *HUSTLERS* (2019)

CONFIT CHICKEN WINGS WITH CHAMPAGNE CRÈME FRAÎCHE

YIELD: 40 WINGS
ALLERGY: DAIRY
TOOL: BUTCHER'S TWINE

Named for the order placed by a patron in the strip club where the majority of the movie takes place. The "on the side" is a Champagne-inspired (as in the drink and the room) dipping sauce for the chicken wings. These wings pair well with a bottle of Champagne.

FOR THE CONFIT CHICKEN WINGS

5 pounds chicken wings

2 quarts canola or vegetable oil

6 tablespoons fresh thyme

1 tablespoon chipotle powder

1 tablespoon smoked paprika

1 ounce dried guajillo pepper

3 tablespoons peeled and crushed garlic

1½ tablespoons kosher salt

2 tablespoons + 1 teaspoon freshly ground black pepper

FOR THE CHAMPAGNE CRÈME FRAÎCHE

1½ tablespoons fresh thyme

½ cup + 1½ teaspoons Prosecco

4 tablespoons finely chopped shallot

2 tablespoons finely chopped garlic

1⅓ cups crème fraîche

2 tablespoons sliced fresh chives

Scant ⅓ cup chopped fresh parsley

½ teaspoon salt

2½ teaspoons Champagne vinegar

FOR THE SEASONING DRY MIX

Scant ¼ cup light brown sugar

3 tablespoons smoked paprika

¾ cup dried oregano

1½ tablespoons cayenne pepper

2 tablespoons + 2 teaspoons kosher salt

4 tablespoons Old Bay seasoning

2 tablespoons chili powder

1½ tablespoons chipotle powder

1 tablespoon onion powder

2½ teaspoons garlic powder

2 tablespoons + 1 teaspoon freshly ground black pepper

FOR FRYING

3 quarts canola or vegetable oil

TO MAKE THE CONFIT WINGS

1. Preheat the oven to 275°F.

2. Place the chicken wings in a roasting pan with all the remaining confit ingredients.

3. Cover tightly with foil.

4. Roast for about 2 hours, or until the wings reach an internal temperature of 165°F.

TO MAKE THE CHAMPAGNE CRÈME FRAÎCHE

1. Tie the thyme, using butcher's twine.

2. Combine the Prosecco with the thyme bundle, shallot, and garlic in a nonreactive saucepan and reduce over medium heat until almost evaporated. Remove from the heat, remove the thyme bundle, and let the Prosecco cool completely.

CONTINUED ▶

3. Whisk together the crème fraîche, cooled Prosecco, chives, and parsley in a nonreactive bowl. Season with the salt.

4. Finish by whisking in the Champagne vinegar.

TO MAKE THE SEASONING DRY MIX

Combine all the seasonings in a bowl and mix well.

TO FRY AND SERVE

1. Heat the oil to 350°F in a large, deep pot.

2. Cook the wings until they reach your desired crispiness.

3. Remove the wings and toss in the seasoning dry mix. Serve with the Champagne crème fraîche on the side.

Janet Jackson's song in the opening was always a part of the script. "This is a story about control. I had written into the script, 'Janet Jackson voice-over.' So incredibly grateful that she gave us the rights to use this song," stated writer-director Lorene Scafaria. Jennifer Lopez was also a backup dancer for Janet Jackson in the '90s.

GOOD MORNING, MR. BREAKFAST

PEE-WEE'S BIG ADVENTURE (1985)

CEREAL-INFUSED WHISKEY, MAPLE SYRUP, LEMON, ORANGE, EGG WHITE, STRAWBERRY, BACON

YIELD: 1 SERVING
GLASSWARE: COUPE GLASS

I pity the poor fool who doesn't try this reimagining of Pee-wee's breakfast machine.

- 2 ounces Mr. T Cereal—Infused Whiskey (recipe follows)
- 0.5 ounce pure maple syrup
- 0.5 ounce fresh lemon juice
- 0.5 ounce fresh orange juice
- 1 egg white
- 1 strawberry for garnish
- 1 strip crisp cooked bacon for garnish

1. Combine all the ingredients, except for the garnishes, in a cocktail shaking tin and shake vigorously without ice.
2. Add ice and shake again.
3. Strain through a fine-mesh strainer into a chilled coupe glass.
4. Garnish with a strawberry and a strip of crispy bacon on the rim.

MR. T CEREAL—INFUSED WHISKEY   YIELD: 750 MILLILITERS

- One 750-milliliter bottle whiskey
- 2 cups Mr. T Cereal (Cap'n Crunch is an adequate substitution if you are unable to find the real thing)

1. Combine the whiskey and cereal in a large bowl and let sit for 2 to 4 hours until cereal is soggy.
2. Strain the whiskey back into the bottle.

After making his first TV appearance on an HBO *Young Comedians* special, Pee-wee Herman made his feature film debut in *Cheech and Chong's Next Movie* (1980) as a rude hotel clerk, then appearing onstage in the film as Pee-wee Herman.

STAFF PICKS:

A CURATED ENDCAP STRAIGHT FROM THE VHS DAYS

With the availability of movies through streaming, ultimately making this book possible, we still think fondly of the 1980s and '90s VHS stores from our youth. We loved the discovery of finding new movies after digging through the store, but during every great expedition, you could always rely on the sage advice of the VHS store clerks too, who curated the endcap of "staff picks" to help guide you. Knowing which staff member's tastes were most like yours—whether it be horror, comedy, action, documentary, or auteur—you inevitably were drawn to a few reliable sources in "staff picks."

PIZZA GENERATION | *PARASITE (2019)*

BULGOGI PIZZA WITH PICKLED PEACHES AND KIMCHI

YIELD: 4 TO 5 (7.5-INCH)
PERSONAL PIZZAS
ALLERGIES: GLUTEN, SOY
TOOLS: ROLLING PIN, GRILL PAN

A Korean-inspired pizza for the Kim family, hard at work folding boxes for Pizza Generation, through fumigation and flood.

FOR THE PIZZA DOUGH

½ cup + 2 tablespoons
   lukewarm water
1½ teaspoons granulated sugar
1¼ teaspoons active dry yeast
2 cups all-purpose flour
½ teaspoon salt
Oil for bowl

FOR THE BULGOGI SAUCE

1 large onion
2 ounces fresh ginger
5½ teaspoons mirin
2 tablespoons + 2 teaspoons
   light brown sugar
8⅓ teaspoons sesame oil

2½ tablespoons
   gochujang paste
1⅓ cups soy sauce
1½ tablespoons water

FOR THE BULGOGI BEEF

1 pound beef (sirloin, flank,
   rib eye, or tenderloin)
1 tablespoon canola oil
½ bunch scallions, thinly sliced
3½ teaspoons white
   sesame seeds

FOR THE PICKLED PEACHES

2 peaches
1 heaping tablespoon
   thinly sliced red onion

½ teaspoon freshly
   ground black pepper
1½ teaspoons mustard seeds
1 cup water
3 tablespoons granulated sugar
⅔ teaspoon salt
5 tablespoons white
   balsamic vinegar

OTHER PIZZA TOPPINGS

12 ounces mozzarella
3 ounces store-bought
   kimchi, roughly chopped
Chopped scallions
Sesame seeds

TO MAKE THE PIZZA DOUGH

1. Combine the water, sugar, and yeast in the bowl of a stand mixer and allow to rest until the yeast has bloomed.

2. Add the flour and salt to the bowl and mix on low speed for 7 minutes with the dough hook.

3. Remove from the mixer and place in a well-oiled bowl. Cover with plastic wrap and allow to rise until the dough has doubled in size.

4. Portion into 3-ounce balls onto a parchment-lined baking sheet. Cover with plastic wrap and transfer to the refrigerator.

TO MAKE THE BULGOGI

1. Peel the onion and ginger, then cut into large chunks.

2. Combine all the bulgogi ingredients in a blender and blend until smooth. Do not strain.

CONTINUED ▶

TO MAKE THE BULGOGI BEEF

1. Thinly slice the beef against the grain.

2. Place a large skillet over medium to high heat. Heat the oil until it begins to smoke slightly. Add the beef strips—be careful not to overcrowd the pan, working in batches, if necessary—and sear.

3. When cooked halfway through, add 5 tablespoons of the bulgogi sauce, toss well, and cook through.

4. Add the scallions and sesame seeds and stir. Small batches require less than 5 minutes total cook time to retain tenderness.

TO MAKE THE PICKLED PEACHES

1. Pit and slice each peach into 12 slices.

2. Combine the sliced peaches and red onion in a 2-quart container.

3. Wrap the black pepper and mustard seeds in a piece of cheese-cloth. Place in a nonreactive pot along with the water, sugar, salt, and vinegar. Bring to a boil, then shut off the heat.

4. Let the liquid cool for 3 to 5 minutes, then pour (with the cheesecloth bundle) into the container of peaches and onion.

5. Let sit until the liquid has reached room temperature.

TO ASSEMBLE

1. Preheat the oven to 425°F, placing a sheet pan upside down on an oven rack as it heats.

2. Using a rolling pin, flatten a ball of the pizza dough into a 7½-inch disk.

3. Place a grill pan over high heat. When hot, put the dough in the pan for 5 to 15 seconds (depending how hot the pan is), then lift and rotate the dough by a quarter turn and cook for another 5 to 15 seconds. Remove from the pan.

4. Spread 3 tablespoons of the bulgogi sauce onto the dough and sprinkle 3 ounces of the mozzarella over the top.

5. Scatter 4 ounces of the beef across and cook on the inverted baking sheet for 5 to 7 minutes, until the cheese is browned.

6. Remove and top with 1 ounce of pickled peaches, chopped kimchi, scallions, and sesame seeds.

7. Slice into quarters.

Director Bong Joon-ho used some of his personal experiences as tutor to a rich family's child as inspiration for the script.

JJAPAGURI (RAM-DON) | *PARASITE (2019)*

KOREAN SPICY BLACK BEAN RAMYUN WITH STEAK

YIELD: 2 SERVINGS
ALLERGIES: GLUTEN, FISH, SHELLFISH (SHRIMP), SOY

Jjapaguri is a popular mash-up of two Korean instant ramyuns. In *Parasite*, the inclusion of domestically grown Korean steak, a highly prized and expensive ingredient, highlights the dichotomy between the Kim and Park families.

1 pound Korean Kobe or similarly high-quality sirloin steak

1 tablespoon oil

One 4.23-ounce package Neoguri (Korean spicy udon instant ramyun)

One 4.23-ounce package Chapagetti (Korean black bean instant ramyun)

Thinly sliced scallion for garnish (optional)

Toasted seaweed for garnish (optional)

Sesame seeds for garnish (optional)

1. Cut the steak into bite-size pieces. Heat the oil in a pan and sear the beef to your desired doneness. Remove from the heat and set aside.

2. Bring 4 cups of water to a boil in a large saucepot. Add the contents of the dried vegetable packets from both ramyun packages as well as the Neoguri soup packet.

3. Add the noodles from both packages. Cook for 3 minutes—the noodles should still be slightly undercooked.

4. Remove from heat and drain most of the soup, leaving about ½ cup in the pot.

5. Return the pot to low heat. Add the contents of the soup packet and the olive oil packet from the Chapagetti package and mix thoroughly.

6. Toss the steak with the noodles and divide between two serving bowls. Top with thinly sliced scallions, toasted seaweed, or sesame seeds, if desired.

DONUT TIME | *TANGERINE (2015)*

ROSEMARY CAKE DONUT WITH TANGERINE AND VANILLA CARAMEL GLAZE

YIELD: 12 DONUTS
ALLERGIES: DAIRY, EGG, GLUTEN
TOOL: DONUT CUTTER

Donut Time was a haunt for LA sex workers, especially transgender sex workers, until it closed in 2016. This is the ultimate comfort food for a messy breakup.

FOR THE DONUTS

2 tablespoons (¼ stick) unsalted butter, at room temperature

1 cup sugar

3 large eggs

4 cups all-purpose flour, plus more for dusting

1 tablespoon baking powder

½ teaspoon salt

1 teaspoon ground cinnamon

¾ cup whole milk

4 cups canola oil for frying

FOR THE GLAZE

1 cup sugar

Water, as needed

Zest and juice of 3 tangerines

Zest and juice of 1 orange

½ cup heavy cream

TO MAKE THE DONUTS

1. Beat together the butter and sugar in a large bowl until sandy in texture. Add the eggs, one at a time, mixing until fully incorporated before adding the next.

2. Combine flour, baking powder, salt, and cinnamon in a medium bowl.

3. Add the milk and the flour mixture to the butter mixture, alternating between them, and mix well.

4. Cover the dough with plastic wrap and place in the refrigerator to let rest for a minimum of 30 minutes.

TO MAKE THE GLAZE

1. While the dough rests, combine the sugar and enough water to loosen the sugar in a heavy-bottomed saucepot. Create a caramel by cooking over medium heat, stirring occasionally, until dark brown.

2. Once the caramel is dark brown, remove from the heat and add the tangerine and orange juice (reserve the zest for now) as well as the cream. Place the pot back over the heat and cook until well combined again.

3. Remove from the heat and stir in the tangerine and orange zest. Let cool to room temperature.

TO FRY AND ASSEMBLE

1. On a well-floured surface, roll out the dough until roughly ¼ inch thick. Cut out donuts using a donut cutter.

2. Heat the oil to 375°F in a tall-sided 4-quart saucepot and fry the donuts in batches until golden brown, flipping halfway through. Place on a wire rack set rack over a cookie sheet.

3. Once the donuts have been fried, carefully dip into the tangerine glaze and return to the rack, glaze side up.

CONTINUED ▶

Tangerine director Sean Baker, a native of Summit, New Jersey, is also the cocreator of the Fox TV series *Greg the Bunny*.

THE CHAROLASTA MANIFESTO

Y TU MAMÁ TAMBIÉN (2001)

TUNA TOSTADA, CILANTRO, AVOCADO PUREE, GRAPEFRUIT VINAIGRETTE

YIELD: 12 TOSTADAS
ALLERGIES: FISH, POSSIBLY GLUTEN (CHECK TORTILLA LABEL)

The road trip from Mexico City to the coast goes through the heart of Mexico. This recipe combines the best of the Pacific coast, where the trip ends, with the refined food of Mexico City.

FOR THE AVOCADO PUREE

2 ripe medium Hass avocados

2 tablespoons fresh lime juice

½ teaspoon Valentina hot sauce

1 teaspoon kosher salt

2 tablespoons extra virgin olive oil

FOR THE GRAPEFRUIT MEZCAL VINAIGRETTE

¼ cup fresh grapefruit juice

2 tablespoons mezcal

½ cup extra virgin olive oil

Salt and freshly ground black pepper

FOR THE TOSTADAS

One 10-ounce package yellow corn tortillas

1 tablespoon canola oil

6 ounces very fresh tuna loin

Fresh cilantro leaves

TO MAKE THE AVOCADO PUREE

1. Remove the avocado from the skin and put into a blender along with the lime juice, hot sauce, and salt. Blend until smooth.

2. Slowly drizzle in the olive oil until fully incorporated.

3. Transfer to a resealable plastic bag or a pastry bag and store in the refrigerator until ready to plate the tostadas.

TO MAKE THE GRAPEFRUIT MEZCAL VINAIGRETTE

Combine all the vinaigrette ingredients in a small bowl, seasoning with salt and pepper. Set aside until needed.

TO MAKE THE TOSTADAS

1. Cut the tortillas with a 2-inch-diameter ring cutter.

2. Heat the canola oil in a skillet and fry the tortillas until crispy on both sides.

3. Remove from the pan and let cool on a cookie sheet lined with paper towels.

4. Slice the tuna into ¼-inch-thick slices.

5. Remove the avocado puree from the refrigerator. If you used a plastic bag, cut off one of the corners so that you will be able to pipe the puree out.

6. Build the tostadas: Starting with the tortilla, pipe out 1 tablespoon of the puree, then top with one slice of the tuna, drizzle some of the vinaigrette on top of the tuna, and finish with a cilantro leaf.

CONTINUED ▶

> Mezcal is made from the heart of the agave plant, the piña, which is roasted over coals for up to a week. Most mezcal comes from the Mexican state of Oaxaca.

The last names of all the principal characters (Zapata, Iturbide, Carranza, etc.) are those of important figures in Mexican history: Emiliano Zapata, Agustín de Iturbide, and Venustiano Carranza. The last name of the one Spanish character—Cortés—is that of the Spanish conquistador Hernán Cortés, who conquered much of Mexico for Spain.

THE AGE OF BLOSSOMS

IN THE MOOD FOR LOVE (2000)

SCOTCH, OOLONG TEA, SESAME SYRUP, LEMON

YIELD: 1 SERVING
GLASSWARE: COLLINS GLASS

The name is taken from the translation of the Chinese title, a Chinese metaphor for the fleeting time of youth, beauty, and love. This cocktail is a nod to the tea that Mrs. Chan drinks throughout the movie, in a collins glass with tulips painted around it.

2 ounces strongly brewed oolong tea

2 ounces Scotch

0.75 ounce Sesame Syrup (recipe follows)

0.5 ounce fresh lemon juice

Food-grade tulip blossom for garnish, if available (optional)

1. Allow the brewed tea to cool completely.
2. Combine all the ingredients, except the garnish, in an ice-filled shaking tin.
3. Shake and strain over an ice-filled collins glass.
4. Garnish with the tulip blossom.

SESAME SYRUP   YIELD: 1½ CUPS

6 ounces sesame seeds

1½ cups water

1¾ cups sugar

1. Toast the sesame seeds in a small saucepan over medium-high heat until they start to slightly brown.
2. Add the water and sugar, bring to a boil, then lower the heat to a simmer and cook for 10 minutes.
3. Remove from the heat and allow to cool completely, then strain.

This film is the fifth of seven collaborations between Wong Kar-wai and cinematographer Chris Doyle.

Oolong tea is a Chinese style of partially oxidized tea. Unlike black teas, which are fully oxidized, or green teas, where the oxidation process is stopped, oolong varieties are carefully manipulated to achieve a specific level of oxidation— somewhere between 8 percent and 85 percent, depending on the type.

Orgeat syrup is a sweet syrup made from almonds, sugar, and rosewater or orange flower water. It was originally made with a barley-almond blend. It usually has a pronounced almond taste and is used to flavor many cocktails. Orgeat syrup is an important ingredient in the Mai Tai and many tiki drinks.

"BLUE" | *MOONLIGHT (2016)*

RUM, MORE RUM, CRÈME DE MÛRE, LIME, CUBAN FRIJOLE ORGEAT, LUSTER DUST

YIELD: 1 SERVING
ALLERGY: TREE NUTS (ALMOND)
GLASSWARE: COUPE GLASS

In Liberty City, Miami, drug dealer and mentor Juan tells a young Chiron ("Little") about growing up in Cuba, how he would run at night and an old Cuban lady would say that the moonlight reflected off his skin, making it look blue. Toward the end of the film, Chiron (now called "Black") is comforted by an old friend and remembers himself as Little, standing on a beach in the moonlight. This cocktail combines the vibrant Cuban heritage of Miami with the soothing color of moonlight.

1.25 ounces Havana Club 7 Años Rum

0.75 ounce Cuban Frijole Orgeat (recipe follows)

0.5 ounce fresh lime juice

0.33 ounce crème de mûre

1 barspoon Cruzan Black Strap Rum

1. Combine all the ingredients in an ice-filled mixing tin.
2. Shake vigorously for 5 to 10 seconds. Double strain into a chilled coupe glass and serve immediately.

CUBAN FRIJOLE ORGEAT YIELD: 15 SERVINGS

¾ cup demerara sugar

¾ cup blue agave nectar

1½ cups water

1 pound dried black beans

1 bunch cilantro

2 garlic cloves, smashed (not chopped)

2 heaping barspoons edible luster dust

1. Combine the demerara sugar, agave, and water into a large pot and bring to a boil, stirring occasionally.
2. Add the dried black beans and cook for 5 minutes, stirring to incorporate.
3. Right before turning off the heat, add the whole bunch of cilantro and the smashed garlic.
4. Cover with a lid and infuse at room temperature for at least 6 hours, but ideally overnight.
5. The next day, reheat the mixture and let simmer over medium heat for 5 to 10 minutes.
6. Strain out all of the aromatics and let cool.
7. Finally, add the luster dust, stir to incorporate thoroughly, bottle, and refrigerate.

CONTINUED ▷

Composer Nicholas Britell applied the slowed-down "chopped and screwed" hip-hop remix technique invented by Houston, Texas's DJ Screw to the orchestral score of *Moonlight*.

FITZCARRALDO | *FITZCARRALDO (1982)*

PISCO, YERBA MATÉ ORGEAT, LIME, EGG WHITE, BITTERS

YIELD: 1 SERVING
ALLERGIES: EGG, TREE NUTS
(ALMOND, MACADAMIA)
GLASSWARE: COUPE GLASS
TOOLS: FOOD PROCESSOR, NUT
BAG (OPTIONAL)

As the movie is set in Peruvian Amazonia, this is a riff on the classic Peruvian Pisco Sour, with the addition of an Amazonian-themed Macadamia Yerba Maté Orgeat.

2.5 ounces Pisco

**1 ounce Macadamia Yerba
Maté Orgeat (recipe follows)**

0.75 ounce fresh lime juice

1 egg white

3 dashes Angostura Bitters

1. Combine all ingredients, except the bitters, in a cocktail shaking tin and shake vigorously without ice.

2. Add ice and shake again.

3. Strain through a fine-mesh strainer into a chilled coupe glass.

4. Top with the Angostura bitters and make a design with a toothpick.

MACADAMIA YERBA MATÉ ORGEAT YIELD: ABOUT 2 CUPS

9 ounces raw macadamia nuts

**1½ cups unsweetened
yerba maté**

1¾ cups sugar

2 tablespoons vodka

**1 teaspoon orange flower
water (optional)**

1. Toast the macadamia nuts in a dry skillet and rinse once with water.

2. Combine the nuts and yerba maté in a food processor and puree. Allow to steep for 3 hours, then strain through a nut bag or fine-mesh strainer.

3. Combine the strained liquid with the sugar in a medium saucepan and bring to a gentle boil.

4. Remove from the heat and add the vodka and orange flower water, if using.

5. Store in an airtight container in the refrigerator for up to 2 weeks.

CONTINUED ▷

Klaus Kinski, despite this being his fourth collaboration with Werner Herzog, fought violently with the crew and raged over trivial matters. The Peruvian natives in particular were very upset about his behavior. Herzog has claimed that one of the chieftains offered, in all seriousness, to murder Kinski for Herzog.

LET YOUR SOUL GLO

COMING TO AMERICA (1988)

BOURBON, GRAPEFUIT AND PASSION FRUIT SYRUP, SELTZER, THYME

YIELD: 1 SERVING
GLASSWARE: HIGHBALL GLASS

When the airline loses your luggage on your flight from Zamunda, you might order this while you're killing time at the airport bar. And don't worry, a couple of these will have you feeling "silky smooth" in no time.

1.25 ounces bourbon or rye whiskey
1.33 ounces Soul Glo Syrup (recipe follows)
3.5 ounces seltzer
Thyme sprig for garnish
Sliced grapefruit for garnish

1. Add all the ingredients, except the garnishes, to your highball glass, add ice to the top, and stir to mix well.

2. Slap the thyme sprig to release the aromatics, and garnish the drink with the thyme and a thin grapefruit peel.

SOUL GLO SYRUP   **YIELD:** 10 TO 12 SERVINGS

1 cup grapefruit juice
1¼ cups + 2½ tablespoons sugar
6 tablespoons passion fruit puree
4 sprigs thyme

1. Combine the grapefruit juice, sugar, and passion fruit puree in a nonreactive saucepot, bring it to a boil, then lower the heat to medium and simmer for 5 to 10 minutes.

2. Right before turning off the heat, add the thyme, stir, and then turn off the heat.

3. Once the syrup is cool, remove and discard the thyme sprigs, bottle, and refrigerate.

BARRY LYNDON | *BARRY LYNDON (1975)*

GIN, PAMPLEMOUSSE, EARL GREY SYRUP, LEMON, LACTIC ACID, EGG WHITE, SMOKED TEA SALT

YIELD: 1 SERVING
ALLERGY: EGG
GLASSWARE: ROCKS GLASS
TOOL: MORTAR AND PESTLE

This floral and aristocratic cocktail is inspired by the atmosphere of the Seven Years War setting of the film.

---

2 ounces Plymouth Gin

0.5 ounce pamplemousse grapefruit liqueur

0.5 ounce Earl Grey Tea Syrup (recipe follows)

0.5 ounce fresh lemon juice

1 dropperful (about 1 ml) lactic acid

1 egg white

Lapsang Tea Salt (recipe follows) for rim

Food-grade rose petal for garnish

1. Combine all the ingredients, except for the tea salt and garnish, into a cocktail shaking tin and shake vigorously without ice.

2. Add ice and shake again.

3. Rim a chilled rocks glass with the lapsang tea salt and add a large ice cube.

4. Strain the cocktail through a fine-mesh strainer into the rocks glass.

5. Garnish with a rose petal.

CONTINUED ▶

EARL GREY TEA SYRUP   YIELD: 1 CUP

1 cup + 2 tablespoons sugar

1 cup water

2 ounces Earl Grey tea leaves

1. Combine all the ingredients in a saucepot. Bring to a boil, then turn off the heat.

2. Allow to steep for 20 minutes, then strain.

LAPSANG TEA SALT   YIELD: 3 TABLESPOONS

1 tablespoon lapsang souchong tea leaves

2 tablespoons kosher salt

Grind the lapsang souchong tea with a mortar and pestle and combine with the kosher salt.

CUP O' PIZZA | *THE JERK (1979)*

TOMATO SOUP, GARLIC CROSTINI, MOZZARELLA, PEPPERONI

YIELD: 4 SERVINGS
ALLERGIES: DAIRY, GLUTEN
TOOL: CIRCULAR CUTTER

They never really explain what a cup of pizza is in the movie, though they discuss which is better: Cup o' Pizza or pizza in a cup. We made a turn on a French onion soup that is essentially pizza in a cup. It will run that old Cup o' Pizza guy out of business.

FOR THE TOMATO SOUP
¼ cup olive oil
10 ounces sweet onion, sliced
3 garlic cloves, chopped
1 tablespoon balsamic vinegar
1 tablespoon salt
1 teaspoon freshly
  ground black pepper
2 tablespoons dried oregano
One 28-ounce can diced
  and peeled tomatoes
⅛ teaspoon baking soda

FOR THE CROSTINI
1 slice bread per serving
1 garlic clove, minced
½ pound (2 sticks) unsalted
  butter, at room temperature
1 cup olive oil

FOR ASSEMBLY
Shredded mozzarella
Sliced pepperoni

> A small amount of baking soda in canned tomatoes removes the tin can flavor.

TO MAKE THE TOMATO SOUP

1. Heat the oil in a medium, nonreactive pot until almost smoking.
2. Add the onion and garlic and cook until caramelized.
3. Deglaze with the balsamic vinegar.
4. Add the salt, pepper, and oregano; stir until the oregano is fragrant.
5. Add the tomatoes and baking soda.
6. Bring to a boil, then lower the heat and simmer for 10 minutes.
7. Remove from the heat and let cool before blending in a blender or with an immersion blender.

TO MAKE THE CROSTINI

1. Preheat the oven to 275°F.
2. Cut each piece of bread into a disk ¼ inch smaller than your individual heatproof serving bowl.
3. Mix together the garlic, butter, and olive oil in a bowl and spread over each disk of bread.
4. Place the bread in the oven and bake for 8 minutes, or until toasted.

TO ASSEMBLE

1. Preheat the oven to BROIL.
2. Place each heatproof bowl on a baking sheet and fill with the tomato soup to ½ inch below the rim.
3. Float a crostini on top of each bowl.
4. Cover with shredded mozzarella and place pepperoni on top, evenly spaced.
5. Bake on the top rack of the oven until the cheese is melted and bubbly and the pepperoni is crispy around the edges.

CONTINUED ▶

The Jerk had a television film sequel, *The Jerk, Too* (1984), starring Mark Blankfield as Navin and costarring Stacey Nelkin. It was executive produced, but not written, by Steve Martin.

T. E. LAWRENCE | *LAWRENCE OF ARABIA* (1962)

GIN, POMEGRANATE, LIME, TONIC, SUMAC

YIELD: 1 SERVING
GLASSWARE: COLLINS GLASS

Gin and tonic, the preferred drink of the British military, is bolstered here with flavors from the Arabian Peninsula.

1.5 ounces London dry gin
0.75 ounce pomegranate juice
0.25 ounce fresh lime juice
4 ounces tonic water
Ground sumac for garnish

1. Pour all the ingredients, except the sumac, over ice into a collins glass.
2. Stir, then top with a pinch of ground sumac.

While shooting Peter O'Toole and I. S. Johar riding together on a single camel, Sir David Lean saw that they had trouble staying on the animal. On closer inspection, a large block of hashish was discovered. Both actors were completely stoned. Shooting was abandoned for the day.

LAST ACTION HERO | *LAST ACTION HERO* (1993)

RYE BOURBON, SCOTCH, TRUFFLE POPCORN SYRUP, EGG WHITE, LEMON, ALLSPICE BITTERS, LIQUID SMOKE

YIELD: 1 SERVING
ALLERGIES: DAIRY, EGG, PEANUTS
GLASSWARE: ROCKS GLASS
TOOL: ATOMIZER, CANDY THERMOMETER

What better than watching the newest Jack Slater movie before it's been released? Watching it with a cocktail in hand, with hints of tobacco and Orpheum's famous buttered popcorn in this tasty whiskey sour riff.

1 ounce high rye bourbon (Redemption High Rye Bourbon recommended)

0.5 ounce blended Scotch (Black Bottle Blended Scotch Whiskey recommended)

1 ounce Truffle Butter Popcorn Syrup (recipe follows)

1 egg white

0.5 ounce fresh lemon juice

1 dash allspice bitters (Dale DeGroff's Pimento Aromatic Bitters recommended)

Spritz of liquid smoke

Caramel Popcorn (recipe follows) for garnish

1. Add the rye bourbon, Scotch, Truffle Butter Popcorn Syrup, egg white, lemon juice, and bitters to a cocktail shaker and shake without ice to emulsify the egg white for 10 seconds.

2. Add ice and shake to chill.

3. Strain into a rocks glass and spritz the top of the cocktail with the liquid smoke using the atomizer.

4. Garnish with caramel popcorn.

TRUFFLE BUTTER POPCORN SYRUP YIELD: 12 TO 15 SERVINGS

2 cups water

1 pound demerara sugar

1 bowl Truffle Shuffle Popcorn (page 242)

1. Bring the water and demerara sugar to a boil in a large pot, then add the truffle popcorn.

2. Lower the heat to a simmer and cook the popcorn in the syrup for 5 minutes.

3. Strain out the popcorn and leave the syrup in the fridge overnight.

4. The next morning, the butter will have solidified. Strain the syrup, discarding the butter.

CONTINUED ▷

CARAMEL POPCORN YIELD: 8 CUPS

8 cups popped popcorn
½ cup sugar
**1½ tablespoons light
corn syrup**
**4 tablespoons (½ stick)
unsalted butter**
1½ teaspoons baking soda
¼ tablespoon kosher salt

1. Put the popped popcorn in a large, heatproof bowl and set aside.

2. Combine the sugar, corn syrup, and butter in a 2-quart saucepot and place over medium heat. Stirring often and using a candy thermometer, cook until the temperature reaches 300°F. Remove from the heat and stir in the baking soda and salt.

3. While the caramel is still hot, gently pour over the popcorn and stir to coat all of the popcorn.

4. Lay out on a clean surface and let cool completely. Break up into small pieces and store in an airtight container.

A rare misfire for Schwarzenegger, *Last Action Hero* has gained a loyal following since its initial release. Filming continued until the week before this movie debuted in theaters, leaving no time for fine-tuning.

KEY ZEST | *THE BEACH BUM (2019)*

COCONUT CALAMARI, SPICY KEY LIME AIOLI

YIELD: 4 SERVINGS
ALLERGIES: SHELLFISH, POSSIBLY SOY (CHOOSE SOY-FREE MAYO, IF NEEDED)
TOOLS: FOOD PROCESSOR (OPTIONAL), SLOTTED SPOON

This take on fried calamari, the trusty beach bar standard, is full of all the flavors of the Florida Keys. Good vibes guaranteed.

FOR THE CALAMARI

1 pound fresh or frozen squid rings and tentacles

One 16-ounce can coconut milk

2 cups fine cornmeal

¾ cup fine dried unsweetened coconut flakes

1 teaspoon salt, plus more for seasoning

1 teaspoon freshly ground black pepper

Pinch of cayenne pepper

Sunflower or other high-heat oil for frying

Lime zest (optional) for garnish

FOR THE SAUCE

Zest and juice of 2 to 3 Key limes

1 cup mayonnaise

1 seeded and finely chopped habanero pepper

1 teaspoon salt

1 teaspoon sugar

⅛ teaspoon freshly grated nutmeg

TO MAKE THE CALAMARI

1. Combine the squid and coconut milk in a medium bowl and allow to soak for at least 30 minutes and up to 3 hours.

2. Combine the cornmeal, dried coconut (if the pieces are too large, pulse in a food processor until they are the texture of panko), salt, black pepper, and cayenne in a large bowl and stir until well mixed.

3. Remove the squid from the coconut milk, using a slotted spoon, and toss in the cornmeal mixture until well coated. Transfer to a mesh strainer and shake to remove any excess cornmeal.

4. Fill a Dutch oven or similar heavy-bottomed pot with 2 inches of high-heat oil. Heat to 350°F and fry the squid until golden brown and crispy, about a minute and a half. Fry in small enough batches that the squid pieces are not crowded and are able to float freely in the oil. Be careful not to overcook the squid, as it becomes tough quite easily.

5. Transfer to a paper towel to drain and season well with salt. Grate some lime zest on top if you want a little extra kick.

TO MAKE THE SAUCE

Finely mince the lime zest and combine with the remaining ingredients. If you are sensitive to spices, add the habanero a bit at a time at the end, testing as you go until you reach your desired spice level.

CONTINUED ▷

This is the second Harmony Korine movie to star an actor from *High School Musical*; the first was *Spring Breakers*, starring Vanessa Hudgens, and *The Beach Bum* stars Zac Efron.

PINK NIGHTMARE | *A CHRISTMAS STORY* (1983)

PINK SNOBALLS OF CHOCOLATE CAKE, MARSHMALLOW FROSTING, SHREDDED COCONUT

YIELD: 12 SERVINGS
ALLERGIES: DAIRY, GLUTEN
TOOLS: CIRCULAR CUTTER, FOOD PROCESSOR

The fluffy and bright neon pink bunny suit that Aunt Clara gifts Ralphie puts in mind the one-of-a-kind Hostess Snoball, with its died pink coconut covering. The fondant ears and eyes complete the look of this pink nightmare.

FOR THE CHOCOLATE CUPCAKES

1⅓ cups water

½ pound + 7 tablespoons unsalted butter

¾ cup unsweetened cocoa powder

6 ounces semisweet chocolate

1 tablespoon vanilla extract

2 cups dark brown sugar

⅔ teaspoon salt

1 large egg

1 large egg yolk

1 cup + 2 teaspoons all-purpose flour, plus more for pan

Scant tablespoon baking powder

Cooking spray for pan

FOR THE MARSHMALLOW TOPPING

2¼ cups water

Four 0.25-ounce packets powdered gelatin

1¾ cups + 2 tablespoons light corn syrup

5 cups + 1½ tablespoons sugar

1 teaspoon salt

1 tablespoon vanilla extract

FOR THE DECORATION

1 pound shredded coconut

Red gel food coloring

Black gel food coloring

10 ounces fondant

TO MAKE THE CHOCOLATE CUPCAKES

1. Preheat the oven to 350°F.

2. Bring the water to a simmer in a large saucepot.

3. Whisk in the butter, cocoa powder, chocolate, vanilla, brown sugar, and salt.

4. Remove from the heat and allow to cool, then whisk in the egg and egg yolk.

5. Combine the flour and baking powder in a stand mixer fitted with the paddle attachment.

6. While beating on medium speed, slowly add the chocolate mixture.

7. Grease and flour a 12-well cupcake pan.

8. Pour the batter into each well, filling to ¼ inch below the top.

9. Bake for 18 minutes, or until the sides pull away from the pan and a toothpick inserted into a cupcake comes out clean.

TO MAKE THE MARSHMALLOW TOPPING

1. Place ½ cup plus 2 tablespoons of the water in a small bowl and add the gelatin. Set aside to bloom.

2. Combine the remaining water, corn syrup, and sugar in a saucepot and bring to a boil.

3. Remove from the heat and allow to cool slightly, then stir in the gelatin mixture.

4. Let cool completely, then put into the cleaned stand mixer fitted with whisk attachment.

5. On low speed, whisk in the salt and vanilla.

6. Slowly increase the speed to high. Whisk until fluffy and tripled in volume.

7. Transfer to a piping bag.

CONTINUED ▶

Red food coloring is often made from bugs: cochineal and carmine are made from ground South American *Dactylopius coccus*, an insect that inhabits a type of cactus known as *Opuntia*.

TO DECORATE

1. Place the shredded coconut in a food processor and drip in red food coloring until your desired pink is achieved.

2. Separate the fondant into two 2-ounce balls and one 6-ounce ball.

3. Mix one 2-ounce ball with black food dye until dark. Create eyes and a mouth.

4. Mix other 2-ounce ball with red food coloring to make a dark pink. Make two inner ears.

5. Mix the 6-ounce ball with red food coloring to make a light pink. Make bunny ears.

TO ASSEMBLE

1. Cut a small hole into the bottom of each cupcake.

2. Pipe in some icing into each cupcake.

3. Top each cupcake with the marshmallow icing and let it drip down the sides.

4. Cover each with pink coconut.

5. Once set, cut off any excess icing with a circular cutter and apply more pink coconut to cover.

6. Using a small amount of icing, apply the fondant decorations.

A Christmas Story

N FILM M.G.M. U à DISTRIBUÉ PAR CINÉMA INTERNATIONAL CORPORATION

NO CRUST | *THE FAST AND THE FURIOUS (2001)*

TUNA SALAD, SCALLION, PEA SHOOTS, PICKLED GINGER, WASABI MAYO, BRIOCHE

YIELD: 1 SERVING
ALLERGIES: FISH, GLUTEN

Since the tuna at Toretto's "was crappy yesterday, it was crappy the day before, and guess what? It hasn't changed," we put an LA spin on the classic tuna sandwich. We still serve it as Paul Walker would have wanted it, though: "no crust."

---

5 ounces canned albacore tuna, drained

1 tablespoon soy sauce

1 tablespoon fresh lime juice

1 teaspoon salt

¼ cup mayonnaise

1 tablespoon wasabi powder

½ teaspoon freshly ground black pepper

2 tablespoons chopped pickled ginger

1 tablespoon chopped scallion

1 brioche loaf, sliced in half horizontally

1 ounce pea shoots

1. Mix the tuna, soy sauce, lime juice, and salt together in a bowl.

2. Stir together the mayonnaise, wasabi, and pepper in a small bowl until consistent.

3. Mix the wasabi mayo, pickled ginger, and scallion with the tuna mixture until combined.

4. Scoop onto one side of a brioche, top with pea shoots and finish with other side of the bread.

5. Cut off the crusts.

Neither Michelle Rodriguez nor Jordana Brewster had driver's licenses or even learner's permits before production of the film.

Enjoy with an ice-cold Corona.

BACK OFF, WARCHILD | *POINT BREAK (1991)*

MEZCAL, APEROL, GINGER CORONA SYRUP, LIME, PINEAPPLE

YIELD: 1 SERVING
GLASSWARE: PILSNER GLASS

"Surfing's the source, change your life, swear to God."

2 ounces mezcal

0.75 ounce Aperol

0.5 ounce Ginger Corona
Syrup (recipe follows)

0.5 ounce fresh lime juice

0.5 ounce pineapple juice

Lime wedge for garnish

1. Combine all the ingredients, except the garnish, in an ice-filled cocktail shaking tin.

2. Shake and strain into an ice-filled pilsner glass.

3. Garnish with a lime wedge.

GINGER CORONA SYRUP   **YIELD:** 12 OUNCES

12 ounces Corona beer

1⅔ cups sugar

6 ounces roughly chopped
fresh ginger (no need to peel)

1. Combine all the ingredients in a blender and blend.

2. Transfer to a pot and simmer over low heat for 2 hours.

3. Strain and allow to cool completely.

The beach spot where the football game is played at the beginning of the film is the same spot used for the soccer game in *The Karate Kid* (1984).

FOR RELAXING TIMES, MAKE IT SUNTORY TIME | *LOST IN TRANSLATION (2003)*

VODKA, POMEGRANATE, LIME, SHISO SYRUP, TONIC, SUMAC

YIELD: 1 SERVING
GLASSWARE: COLLINS GLASS

The main character Charlotte drinks vodka tonics throughout the film. We honored her with this Japanese-inspired version to fit with the setting. For relaxing times, make it Suntory time.

1.5 ounces Suntory Haku Vodka

0.75 ounce pomegranate juice

0.25 ounce fresh lime juice

¼ ounce Shiso Syrup
 (recipe follows)

4 ounces tonic water

Pinch of ground sumac

Shiso leaf for garnish

1. Pour all the ingredients, except the sumac and garnish, over ice into a collins glass.

2. Stir, then top with a pinch of ground sumac and a shiso leaf.

SHISO SYRUP **YIELD:** 1 CUP

1 cup + 2 tablespoons sugar

1 cup water

5 shiso leaves

1. Combine the sugar and water in a saucepot and bring to a boil.

2. Turn off the heat, add the shiso leaves, steep for 20 minutes, and then strain.

In 1980, Francis Ford Coppola and Akira Kurosawa collaborated on directing some ads for Suntory Whisky at the Coppolas' home in San Francisco.

After creating (and selling out of) some of the world's most sought-after whiskies, Suntory set its sights on clear spirits. Suntory Haku Vodka, distilled in Kagoshima, Kyushu, is made from 100 percent Japanese white rice. Its name, Haku, is rooted in the Japanese word for white rice, *hakumai*.

Star anise is made from the fruit of the Chinese evergreen tree *Illicium verum*. It's aptly named for the star-shaped pods from which the spice's seeds are harvested and has a flavor that is reminiscent of licorice.

THE TREE OF LIFE | *THE TREE OF LIFE* (2011)

APPLE BRANDY, LEMON JUICE, MAPLE SYRUP, ALLSPICE, STAR ANISE

YIELD: 1 SERVING
GLASSWARE: ROCKS GLASS

Money doesn't grow on trees, but all the ingredients of this drink do. Enjoy this beautiful slow burn.

---

2 ounces Laird's Applejack
0.75 ounce fresh lemon juice
0.5 ounce pure maple syrup
6 to 8 drops (6 to 8 ml) St. Elizabeth Allspice Dram
Star anise for garnish

1. Combine all the ingredients, except the star anise, in a cocktail shaking tin.
2. Shake well and strain over ice into an ice-filled rocks glass.
3. Garnish with star anise.

Following his second film, *Days of Heaven*, Terrence Malick moved to Paris in the summer of 1978 and began work on a project called *Q*, which dramatized the origins of life. This eventually became *The Tree of Life*.

ACKNOWLEDGMENTS

MATTHEW VIRAGH, FOUNDER: Matthew hatched the Nitehawk concept in 2010, based on his passion for cinema and the New York City food and beverage scene. Originally from Texas, Matthew has been a Brooklynite since 2001 and an avid film lover for much longer. One of his earliest cinema memories was seeing *The Goonies* at the local multiplex with his late mother, and he credits both of his parents for fully supporting the pursuit of this road less traveled. Along with the rest of Nitehawk's passionate staff, Matthew wants to ensure every guest is receiving a unique and memorable experience, enhanced by the enjoyment of food and drink during a film.

REBECCA VIRAGH, FOUNDER: Rebecca was a successful art director in the advertising industry for many years until she helped open Nitehawk Cinema with her husband, Matthew, in 2011. Though overqualified, she has cultivated the visual language of Nitehawk (along with Yogi Naraine, who developed the hawk reel logo). Her design expertise and support across all departments has been critical to the development of Nitehawk over the last decade.

JESSICA GIESENKIRCHEN, DIRECTOR OF OPERATIONS: Jessica's restaurant career started at the ripe age of eight while doing inventory for her dad's nightclub in Münster, Germany. While at the Fashion Institute of Technology, she started working as a hostess at the Village Restaurant, where the restaurant life took hold and she moved quickly up the ranks to handling all events and managing the busy West Village establishment. Jess joined Nitehawk before our opening in 2011 as a manager and has been an integral part of the growth and development of what Nitehawk is today.

JOHN WOODS, FILM PROGRAMMER: Nitehawk's Director of Programming and Acquisitions has been involved in music and filmmaking for nearly 30 years. John was also the cofounder and owner of the Reel Life video stores throughout Brooklyn, with the first location opening on Bedford Avenue in 1997. Much like the video store curation, John approaches film and live event programming by making it as inclusive and populist as possible (with a healthy bit of subversion)—or as he believes, "Everyone's taste is valid." John's most recently released feature-length film is *New Breed Documentary 1989*.

CARYN COLEMAN, FILM PROGRAMMER: Caryn is a New York–based film programmer whose work is focused on gender parity in independent film. She's the founder of The Future of Film is Female, an organization that amplifies the work of all female filmmakers through a short film fund, commitment to exhibition, and community-building programs, including an ongoing screening series at the Museum of Modern Art. She's a longtime programmer at Nitehawk Cinema, having been Director of Programming/Special Projects and currently the director of the annual Nitehawk Shorts Festival. Caryn received the 2012 Creative Capital/Warhol Foundation Arts Writers Initiative grant and has organized panels for the Art House Convergence, Nightstream, Athena Film Festival, Connective Conversations for The Ford Family Foundation, and CAA. She is a short film advocate, a horror film lover, and a Delphine Seyrig superfan.

MICHAEL FRANEY, CHEF: Michael was born and raised in the suburbs of Baltimore, Maryland, and started working in kitchens at the age of 20. At 21, he moved to New York City to attend the French Culinary Institute. After graduating, he returned to Baltimore and made his bones under the tutelage of James Beard Award nominee Cindy Wolf, working his way up to sous chef within the Charleston Restaurant Group. He returned to NYC with Kimpton Hotels and Restaurants, helping them open properties in Baltimore and Philadelphia. Michael settled in Brooklyn in 2011 and was fast friends and neighbors with Jessica, Director of Operations at Nitehawk. He became part of the Nitehawk Cinema family in 2012. He currently resides in the Park Slope neighborhood in Brooklyn with his wife, Claire, and son, Bo.

STEWART GARY, CHEF: From the west coast of Canada, Stewart started out in the dish pit of a local fish and chips restaurant. Despite going home each night smelling of tartar sauce and cod, he found his passion. He graduated from South Delta culinary arts program, then worked his way up the ranks of many established restaurants in Vancouver, learning from several of the area's top chefs. Upon moving to New York, he sought out unique and challenging locations to expand his culinary repertoire, with stints as a sous chef at Citi Field with the New York Mets and executive chef at Bloomingdale's with the David Burke Group. Nitehawk has given him a new creative outlet, and he takes great pleasure in pushing the artistic boundaries of popcorn and movie theater cuisine. Stewart no longer smells of tartar sauce and cod.

BLESSING SCHUMER-STRANGE, CHEF: After realizing that he wasn't cut out for cubicle life, Blessing spent his formative culinary years working in high-end New American food in the Bay Area. He joined the Nitehawk family a few years after returning to New York City in order to fully indulge his lifelong love of queso and '80s action flicks. He finds great pleasure in the surprising and wonderful result of creating food for the cinema.

DAVID ZELAYA, CHEF: Born in Honduras and raised in Brooklyn, David is a Le Cordon Bleu graduate and has been in the industry over 13 years. He can also quote *a lot* of movies, in addition to his penchant for developing movie-inspired food recipes.

SAUL BOLTON, CHEF: Saul, opening executive chef of Nitehawk Cinema, was born in Cleveland, Ohio. He went on to live in Cincinnati, Ohio; London, England; Augusta, Georgia; Boston, Massachusetts; Palo Alto, California; and Portland, Oregon—finally ending up in Brooklyn, New York, where he has lived with his wife and two sons for the last 16 years. Saul was chef and owner of Michelin-starred Saul Restaurant. He also was chef and partner of the Vanderbilt and Brooklyn Bangers with the Brooklyn Food and Drink Restaurant Group. Three of his favorite movies are *Blazing Saddles*, *The Deer Hunter*, and *The Unforgiven*.

NICK DODGE, BEVERAGE: Hailing from Detroit, Nick has been behind a bar in various capacities for over half his life. As Beverage Director at Nitehawk Cinema, he has enjoyed being at the intersection of food, drink, film, and culture. He loves gory movies, dive bars, making cocktails, and seeing the world.

ROB GILES, BEVERAGE: Since 2015, Rob has been the managing partner for two distinct cocktail bars, Erv's on Beekman and Until Tomorrow, designing seasonal menus that focus on unique flavor combinations. The bars he opened received numerous accolades, including national top 10 lists and a 2018 *Eater* Young Gun nomination. A born-and-bred New Yorker, his restaurant philosophy is about creating convivial public spaces that cater to people of all walks of life. He joined the Nitehawk family in September 2018 as the Beverage Director at Nitehawk Williamsburg.

BAYLEA MORGAN, BEVERAGE: Baylea is a Chicago native and avid movie lover. A theater school graduate turned night owl, she got into the cocktail scene in Chicago. Moving to New York City and working everywhere from a Manhattan five-star to a rooftop cocktail lounge to a tiki bar, she finally landed at the amazing neighborhood dine-in movie theater, Nitehawk. Her love for a good movie reference will always stay strong, and she was overjoyed to be a part of this amazing team and to build such a wonderful guide to making a night at the movies at home!

MATTHEW WALKER, BEVERAGE: Matt is a Vermont native who has worked in the bar and restaurant industry for 20 years. He currently owns and operates Broken Hearts Burger in Fairlee, Vermont. Matt has functioned as a bartender or beverage manager in the fine dining restaurants of the Hamptons, tropical bars in the USVI, and multiple concepts in Brooklyn, where he served as Beverage Director at Nitehawk Cinema for five years. His hobbies include wild food foraging, knot tying, gardening, and obsessively following cat-related Instagram pages.

JEN MARSHALL, BEVERAGE: Jen was born and raised in San Francisco and started her beverage career spending six years at Peet's Coffee. After 10 years in Chicago, she moved to New York City, where she finally landed in the cocktail industry and hasn't looked back since. As the original Beverage Director at Nitehawk Cinema, she created the initial menus and spearheaded some of the first events. After leaving Nitehawk several years later, Jen collaborated on the opening of Butter & Scotch in Brooklyn. She took a leap over to the supplier side of the industry in 2014, taking a job with William Grant & Sons, where she worked with multiple brands (including Milagro Tequila and Montelobos Mezcal). Fast-forward to 2021, she's still working with Casa Lumbre (the parent company in Mexico that created the brands she worked on), focusing solely on their new Mexican spirits. Jen focuses both on sales and trade advocacy/events for work, but also stays active within the community by volunteering for initiatives that help the hospitality community. She loves motorcycles and mezcal negronis (not at the same time), and staying just social enough to justify the hashtag #iknowjenmarshall.

JESSE MARINO, BEVERAGE: Bar Manager at Nitehawk Cinema, Jesse hails from New Jersey and has worked in the bar industry in New York for eight years, since graduating from the University of Delaware's hospitality management program. In his free time, he likes to bring his work home with him by cooking and making drinks to enjoy while watching even more movies.

BENJAMIN ZORN, BEVERAGE: A queer bartender currently based in New York City, their current focus in the industry centers around creating communities around food and drink, and taking a less capitalist approach to bar and restaurant spaces.

DANIEL THOMPSON, BEVERAGE: Daniel moved to Brooklyn in 2007 and in 2011 fell in love with the idea of Nitehawk. It was an honor to serve as the Lead Bartender for nearly three years at the original Nitehawk location (and he also fell in love with his wife, Ryan, there too)! It was a dream come true to be featured in this book!

JEFFREY JACOBS, FILM BOOKER: Our one and only Film Booker, Jeffrey took on our little independent cinema in Brooklyn right at the beginning and was a tireless champion of our brand of cinema to the film distribution world at large. Without his efforts, we would not have been able to become a legitimate independent cinema in a large sea of NYC film exhibition.

LAUREN VOLO, PHOTOGRAPHER: Lauren studied photography at Syracuse University at the School of Visual and Performing Arts in—gasp—a darkroom! Moving to New York City in 2004, she began working in production before she found her footing in assisting one of the top food photographers for many years. In 2012, she began her own business and has since gone on to shoot many cookbooks, as well as working with large and small brands on commercial ad campaigns for social and print media. She lives in North Brooklyn with her husband, two sons, and animal menagerie.

MICHAEL TIZZANO, EDITOR, THE COUNTRYMAN PRESS: Born and raised in New York City, Michael Tizzano has been working with The Countryman Press since 2016. When he goes out to see a movie, he prefers to do so at the Prospect Park location with an old fashioned.

ALLISON CHI, ART DIRECTOR, THE COUNTRYMAN PRESS: Originally from Minnesota, Allison moved to New York City 2012. Prior to joining The Countryman Press, she held positions at Houghton Mifflin Harcourt, Time Inc. Books, and Hachette Book Group. When she's not designing books, you can find her knitting, weaving, or baking fresh sourdough bread.

JARED BARON, FRIEND OF NITEHAWK: A supporter of Nitehawk Cinema since the beginning, Jared is a multi-instrument musician with a baby grand piano in his living room and a penchant for reading Russian literature on the subway. His career in publishing and guidance led to Nitehawk Cinema's book deal with The Countryman Press, and we are forever grateful.

IRENE YOO, FRIEND OF NITEHAWK: The founder and chef of Yooeating, a Korean American comfort food popup that highlights Korean home cooking, street food, and drinking culture. She is a regular contributor to Food52 and the Food Network, among others. Her latest original recipe videos can be found on the Yooeating YouTube channel. Irene was an indispensable resource as we moved from book concept into execution and photography of the book.

ABOUT
NITEHAWK
CINEMA

Nitehawk Cinema is New York's premier dine-in theater, pairing exemplary first-run and repertory film programming along with tableside food and beverage service. Our original Williamsburg location opened in 2011, whereas our Prospect Park location opened in December 2018.

Nitehawk strives to enhance the cinematic experience with a creative framework by providing a specialty menu with fresh, local ingredients inspired by the films we love; archival 35 mm projection; and special guest Q&As.

Nitehawk offers diverse, thoughtful, and engaging programming through our brunch, midnite, and signature series, which honor cinema's past with ongoing repertory screenings and support the future of filmmaking with screenings of new independent films. We strive to reach a wide range of audiences, from the cinephile to the casual movie fan, to encourage exploration of new, lesser-known films and reexperiencing familiar classics in new ways. Making moviegoing special is why we present one-of-a-kind events with screenings featuring filmmakers in person, specialty menus, live performances, and lively discussions. Nitehawk is also committed to promoting local, independent filmmakers by hosting regular screenings of feature films of all genres by diverse filmmakers, screening short films with New York partners, and presenting the annual Nitehawk Shorts Festival. Our mission to change the makeup of representation in the film industry is a driving force throughout our programming as we help new voices emerge in filmmaking.

Nitehawk Williamsburg is a triplex, hosting 92-, 60-, and 34-seat theaters. Lo-Res, Nitehawk's downstairs bar, offers full-service food and drink, provides outdoor seating during the warmer months, provides features handcrafted cocktails, local brews, and spirits from regional distillers. There's also a 24/7 loop of our digitized VHS collection called the VHS Vault.

Nitehawk Prospect Park, our second location, houses seven screens, with theaters ranging in size from 48 to 194 seats. Nitehawk's upstairs bar offers full-service food and drinks, and features handcrafted cocktails, local brews, and spirits from regional distillers.

THE HISTORY OF 188 PROSPECT PARK WEST

One of the oldest buildings in New York that has continuously housed a movie theater, this location originally opened in August 1928 as The Sanders theater with 1,581 seats and a single screen. The Sanders existed until it closed in 1978, and the building sat unoccupied for nearly two decades.

The building was renovated and reopened as the Pavilion Theater in 1996, with three screens, 600 seats, and a café on the second floor. The capacity was eventually expanded to nine screens with 1,350 seats, and the building was included in the 2012 Park Slope Historic District Extension by the Landmarks Preservation Commission.

After closing in 2016, the Pavilion underwent an extensive two-year renovation, reopening in December 2018 as Nitehawk Prospect Park, with seven screens, 650 seats, and in-theater table service as well as two bars. Many original aspects of the Sanders have been preserved, including marble stairs that were hidden beneath carpeting, original plasterwork, and a balcony dating back to the 1920s.

WE CHANGED THE LAW

Setting a historical precedent, Nitehawk Cinema is single-handedly responsible for the groundbreaking overturn of the Prohibition-era New York State liquor law that made serving alcohol in motion picture theaters illegal. Governor Andrew Cuomo signed the new law allowing moviegoers to enjoy an adult beverage at their theater seats a mere three months after the Cinema's opening date; and thus, a new era of boozy film viewing in Brooklyn (and beyond) began!

INDEX

Italics indicate illustrations.